891

1.25

NATURE'S DRINKS

Recipes for Vegetable
and Fruit Juices,
Teas and Coffees

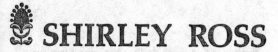

SHIRLEY ROSS

NATURE'S DRINKS

RECIPES FOR VEGETABLE AND FRUIT JUICES, TEAS AND COFFEES

VINTAGE BOOKS
A Division of Random House, New York

The author wishes to acknowledge the cooperation of the following organizations in researching sections of this book:

The Pan American Coffee Bureau
The Tea Council of the U.S.A.

Vintage Books Edition April 1974

Copyright © 1974 by Shirley Ross

All rights reserved under International and Pan-American Copyright Conventions. Published in the United States by Random House, Inc., New York, and simultaneously in Canada by Random House of Canada Limited, Toronto.

Manufactured in the United States of America

Illustrations by Charlotte Staub

❧ CONTENTS

✿ INTRODUCTION

FLAVORED DIETARY BEVERAGE. *Contains carbonated water, citric acid, gum arabic, sodium saccharin, sodium citrate, 1/40 of 1% benzoate of soda and stannous chloride as preservatives, natural and artificial flavorings, salt, glycerol ester of wood rosin, brominated vegetable oil, artificial coloring.*

So reads the label of one of the most popular soft drinks in America, an "imitation citrus flavored dietary artificially sweetened carbonated beverage." Millions of bottles and cans of this product are annually consumed by men, women and children who are not aware that there is another, better and safer way to satisfy their thirst.

This book has been conceived and written as a guide to preparing and serving delicious, energizing, nutritious drinks free of chemical dyes and preservatives, with few calories and no artificial sweetening agents; drinks from the natural laboratory of the earth.

The following pages list and describe many different kinds of safe, healthful beverages: unprocessed raw vegetable- and fruit-juice combinations, blender drinks, brews of coffees and teas.

None of these beverages is "natural" in the narrow,

old-fashioned sense, which limits "nature" by excluding
man, his mind and his products. All the drinks in this book
are human inventions and illustrate the proper use of
technology.

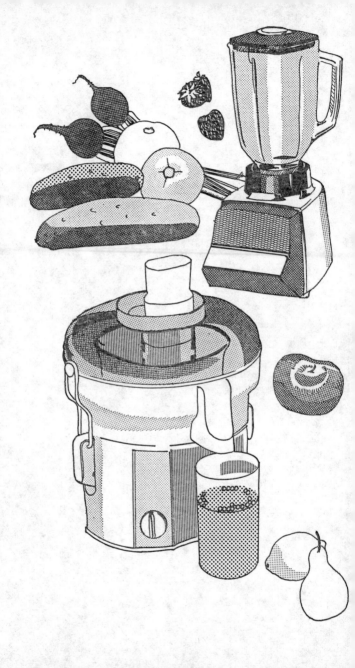

RAW
VEGETABLE
AND FRUIT
DRINKS

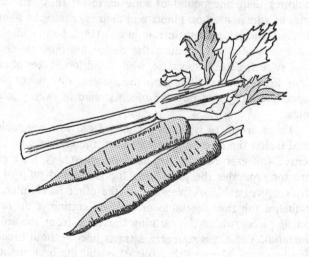

Among the very important reasons for drinking raw juices are, first, that excessive heat, as in cooking, destroys the vitamins, minerals, trace elements and enzymes; second, raw vegetable and fruit juices contain more energy-giving qualities and fewer calories per ounce than any other natural food source (for example, eight ounces of carrot juice is more nutritional and contains far fewer calories than one pound of solid carrots); third, the injurious sprays used on plants find their way into the fibers but not the juices; fourth, raw juices, taken before meals, have a tendency to reduce the desire for fats, starches and sweets, partially because, while solid food takes about four hours to assimilate into the system, raw juices are completely digested into the blood stream in twenty minutes.

There are three ways to get juice from raw vegetables and fruits: the electric juice extractor, the blender and the citrus squeezer (electric or hand operated). A juice extractor separates the juice from the fibers and pulp of a fruit or vegetable. A blender, on the other hand, merely liquefies the raw vegetable or fruit by cutting it up into small pieces without separating the juice from the solid material. The citrus squeezer extracts juice without breaking apart the fibers of the fruit. It is still the best method for juicing citrus fruits, though it produces less liquid than a juice extractor.

The great advantage that juice extractors have over blenders and squeezers is that they provide valuable nutrients from vegetables and fruits in a form the body can readily assimilate. These nutrients—vitamins, minerals, trace elements, and enzymes—are not found in the pulp and fibers, only in the juices. When the fruit or vegetable is eaten in solid form, some of the juices remain hidden in the fibers, which often cannot be digested by the body and pass through as waste.

JUICERS
BLENDERS
SQUEEZERS

There are several kinds of machines which are used for juice extraction, each with its own advantages and disadvantages:

CENTRIFUGAL FORCE JUICERS This is the ideal type of juicing machine for everyday use in the home. Fruits and vegetables are cut up and fed through a slot into a spinning basket which has sides perforated with very small holes. On the bottom of the basket there is a separate cutting blade, a spinning plate with dozens of tiny sharp teeth, which cuts the fruits and vegetables, forcing the pulp and fibers centrifugally against the perforated sides of the basket. The juices run through the holes into an outer bowl surrounding the basket and then down a release spout into a glass or container. The pulp and fibers remain pinned to the sides of the basket in a semi-dry state.

This kind of machine can be bought in models ranging from $50 to $150. The major differences between the $50-to-$100 machines and those over $100 are that the cheaper machines are less efficient in extracting all the juice and thus may in the long run wind up as more expensive because of the cost of fruits and vegetables, and also that the materials in the cheaper machines, particularly the juicing parts, are not made of stainless steel and therefore have a shorter life. In buying a juice extractor, one should look for (1) a capacity to juice at least one quart between cleanings; (2) all-stainless-steel juicing parts; (3) floating cutting blade, also stainless steel; (4) ball-bearing motor allowing for 3,600 revolutions per minute; (5) spring-clutch release (instead of usual nut) holding blade in position, thus allowing easy release for cleaning and avoiding the need for tools; (6) ten-year guarantee on all parts with the exception of the cutting blade.

AUTOMATIC PULP EJECTOR JUICERS   These are similar to the centrifugal force juicers except that the juice is passed through a release spout while the pulp and fibers go out through an exhaust spout. The advantage of this kind of machine is that it allows continuous operation. It does not have to be stopped and cleaned after one quart has been extracted (however, it still has to be cleaned after every use). The disadvantage is that it is less efficient than the centrifugal force machine and does not extract nearly as much juice. These machines are available in the $100 range.

HYDRAULIC PRESSURE JUICERS   These are the best (and most expensive) type of machine, although better suited to restaurant or institutional than to home use. The fruits and vegetables are chopped, broken and shredded into tiny pieces, then hydraulically pressed. The hydraulic press extracts a higher percentage of juice than any of the other machines, leaving behind a very dry "mat" of fibers and pulp. The juice is often so strong that it has to be diluted for drinking. Prices begin at about $350.

THE BLENDER   While the juicer *extracts,* the blender *liquefies* by cutting or chopping the pulp to an extremely fine, liquid blend. The blender transforms solid food into liquid food; the juicer creates a totally different kind of food (drink), which has a chemical and nutritional composition different from that of the solid from which it was extracted.

Still, many really delicious drinks can be prepared in a blender. It is best to follow the operating instructions from the manufacturer for the particular model you own.

THE CITRUS SQUEEZER   The old-fashioned orange-juice squeezers which our mothers used to use have been updated in modern electric versions, which speed and simplify the process. The principle is still the same: to cut a citrus fruit in half and squeeze until every possible drop of juice is removed. Somehow, although the electric squeezers are more convenient, the old-fashioned method still appeals to me. Squeezers should be used for all citrus fruits. The juice from an extractor will be so concentrated it will hardly taste like the familiar "orange juice" or "pineapple juice" we know. Of course, the extractor can be used, but for the familiar flavor, stick to the squeezer.

VITAMINS & MINERALS

Vitamins and minerals are chemicals which ensure the proper functioning of the body's cells. They are not food or nutrients in themselves, but they are essential catalysts in organizing the body's living processes.

Vitamins and minerals cannot be produced within the body. They are best obtained from live foods, where the organic molecular structure is retained intact. Often such elements will be altered or destroyed by contemporary methods of packaging, processing and preserving.

The body contains over twenty minerals, most of which are important to good health. The amount present in the body is sometimes tiny, but the effect is crucial. Vitamins, in a sense, are doubly important, both for their own beneficial activity and because they control the body's utilization of minerals.

With the exception of vitamins A and D, vitamins and minerals are nontoxic even when overdoses are taken, and they can be safely stored in the body or excreted as waste.

VITAMIN A Protects the linings of mucous membrane throughout the body; a fat-soluble vitamin which is stored in the body and therefore open to the possibility of toxic overdose; obtained from carotene, found in carrots and green vegetables; susceptible to oxidation at high temperatures; deficiency results in poor growth, bad teeth and night blindness.

VITAMIN B$_1$ (THIAMINE) Important to the nervous system, prevents beriberi, and aids metabolism and growth; soluble in water, easily destroyed by heat, and excreted through urine; does not store in the body and must be replenished on a daily basis.

VITAMIN B$_2$ (RIBOFLAVIN) This is the one vitamin that is not best taken in raw form, as its catalytic action is much more effective after cooking; found in leafy vegetables; essential for growth.

VITAMIN C (ASCORBIC ACID) Important to blood vessels, tissues, body structure, wound-healing, normal metabolism and prevention and treatment of scurvy; cannot be stored in the body and must be replenished every day; needed in increasing amounts during time of infection (i.e., colds); oxidized by heat and light and exposure to air; totally destroyed in cooked food; found in citrus fruits and green vegetables.

VITAMIN D Known as the sunshine vitamin; a cure for rickets, a bone disease that prevents the body from using its supply of calcium and phosphorus in a normal manner; calcium and phosphorus need the interaction of vitamin D; otherwise they are excreted from the body instead of absorbed through the intestinal walls into the blood to develop teeth and bones. D is a fat-soluble vitamin that is stored in the body and toxic in overdose; nonexistent in plants, its major source is sunlight; another source is cod-liver oil, which can be added to juices in small amounts in winter.

VITAMIN E A controversial vitamin which is claimed to be an antisterility compound and strengthener of the heart; active as an agent in healing fibers; can be obtained from green vegetables but the main source is wheat-germ oil.

CALCIUM A framework and structural material essential to the growth and durability of bones and teeth; constantly needed due to body drain; particularly necessary during the early years and periods of pregnancy and breast-feeding.

CHLORINE Forms hydrochloric acid in the stomach and serves as an antiseptic factor in the system; daily need is large, as the body excretes its daily intake through the urine.

IODINE Utilized in the thyroid gland to produce thyroid hormones (thyroxine), which are important to mental and physical health; must be kept in proper balance, as too much or too little severely upsets the system.

IRON Of primary importance to the supply and condition of red blood cells; carries oxygen through the body; stored in the liver, but a constant supply is needed for creation and replacement of red cells.

MAGNESIUM Essential for muscular tissues, bone structure, nerves and the brain; an important ingredient in chlorophyll, the greening substance found in vegetation; necessary for proper metabolism.

MANGANESE Important aid in sexual functioning, bone formation and tissue respiration; found in green leafy vegetables.

PHOSPHORUS Daily supply needed for good health, especially for proper bone structure, where 90 percent of the body's phosphorus is stored; present in every cell of the body.

POTASSIUM An important regulator of bodily fluids; prominent in tissues and blood cells; united with phosphorus, it aids the brain cells; helps to heal injuries.

SODIUM Helps to determine the amount of water held in the tissues and to keep the proper balance.

VEGETABLES & FRUITS: THE RAW MATERIALS

It is important to remember that raw vegetable and fruit drinks are actually live foods: in the case of juiced vegetables, the raw juice is the vegetable minus pulp and fibers; in the case of a blended fruit, the liquid is simply a permutation of the original form.

Before consulting the recipes in this book, one should be familiar with the ingredients for these drinks. The following "dictionary" is designed to provide handy information—descriptions of various vegetables and fruits, their nutritional values, and instructions for juicing, squeezing, storing and drinking them.

In the following listings, the vitamin amounts refer to the raw food before juicing. They are represented in terms of IU, or international units. The amounts of minerals and trace elements in these foods, though very small, are of great importance. They are listed here only in relative strength. For exact amounts and more detailed information, there is a very good reference guide published by the U.S. Department of Agriculture: *Composition of Foods—Agricultural Handbook #8,* which is sold by the Superintendent of Documents, U.S. Government Printing Office, Washington, D.C. 20402. The price is $2.00.

Many of the recipes call for milk. As an alternative

to cow's milk, use any one of the following combinations,
or if you prefer, goat's milk.

FENNEL MILK

1 cup buttermilk ¼ teaspoon fennel seeds	Blend all ingredients in blender until smooth. Strain if necessary. (Serves 1.)

ALMOND MILK

¼ cup almonds, blanched 2 teaspoons honey 1 cup warm water	Put all ingredients in blender and mix until smooth. Strain if neces- sary. (Serves 1.)

COCONUT MILK

1 cup shredded coconut 1½ teaspoons honey 1 cup warm water pinch salt	Add all ingredients to blender and mix until smooth. Strain if neces- sary. (Serves 1.)

SOYBEAN MILK

1 cup soybeans

Soak the soybeans for 24 to 48 hours in enough water
to cover them. Change the water at least twice a day and
then drain. Place the soaked soybeans in a saucepan with
4 cups of water. Bring to a slow boil. Pour into blender
and mix at low speed until smooth. Strain. This milk is
much more healthful than cow's milk and is a perfect substitute for it. (Serves 4.)

ALFALFA Alfalfa is a leguminous herb with trifoliate leaves and purple flowers. As it is difficult to find this herb in stores, the best way to have a constant supply of fresh alfalfa is to grow it on the window sill. The larger the plant grows, the more trace minerals are sent to the leaves by the ever-enlarging roots. Alfalfa seeds can be purchased at nurseries, dime stores or hardware stores.

Alfalfa juice is too potent to drink undiluted. The best way to drink it is to add at least an equal amount of carrot juice. Use the leaf and the stem for juicing. Four ounces of alfalfa contain 18,000 IU vitamin A, 500 IU vitamin B_2. Alfalfa is also one of the richest sources of chlorophyll, which helps to build up resistance to infection and relieves respiratory trouble.

APPLES Aside from their delicious flavor, apples have several advantages over other fruits. They are available year-round in many different varieties, and they can be stored for weeks or even months at a time if placed in a moisture-tight bag in the refrigerator.

Dozens of varieties of apples are grown in this country. Summer apples are usually more tart than the winter and autumn varieties, which are better for juicing and blending. Among the domestic varieties, the best for drinking are Northern Spy, Baldwin, Yellow Newton and Winesap. McIntosh, Jonathan and York Imperial are much lower in vitamin C. Delicious apples, while among the apples most commonly used for eating, are not recommended for juicing.

Store apples in the refrigerator as close to 32° as possible without freezing. Do not leave at room temperature, as they will lose their crispness very quickly. Periodically check the stored apples and remove those that develop brown spots.

Apples can be juiced or blended. You can use red, yellow or green apples, but bear in mind that "the redder the apple, the sweeter the juice." A single average-sized apple will make about ½ cup of extracted juice. Always use hard, crisp apples for juicing. When blending, it is necessary to remove the peel and core the apple. For the juice extractor you need only wash the fruit with cold water, remove the stem and blossom ends, and cut into small enough pieces to fit into the feeding throat of the juicer.

Apples are rich in magnesium, iron and silicon and contain malic acid, which is an organic element involved in the digestive processes. A medium-sized apple contains 75 IU vitamin A, 23 IU vitamin B_1, 20 IU vitamin B_2 and 200 IU vitamin C. Fresh apple juice can be frozen and used at a later date, or it can be kept for many weeks in a refrigerator if the temperature is cold enough to prevent the juice from fermenting.

APRICOTS Apricots are grown mainly in California, Washington and Utah. Their season is limited to July and August. As it bruises easily and can be injured in shipment, the fresh tree-ripened fruit is not likely to be available outside the western United States. This creates a buying problem because apricots reach full flavor only when tree-ripened.

Purchase plump, juicy fruits with reddish-orange color and avoid small fruits with either hard flesh or greenish coloring; these are immature. Test the fruit with a gentle squeeze. If the fruit is soft, it has begun to go bad. However, a somewhat immature fruit can be ripened at home by placing it in a paper bag at room temperature. When the apricots ripen, put them in the refrigerator.

The best-known varieties of apricots are Alexander, Blenheim and Early Golden, which has fruits almost as large as peaches. All these can be either juiced or blended. In either case, remove the pit and the stems. Apricots are a good source of calcium, phosphorus, iron, sulfur and potassium, and an excellent source of vitamin A. One medium fruit contains 1,840 IU vitamin A, 4 IU vitamin B_1, 16 IU vitamin B_2 and 25 IU vitamin C.

ASPARAGUS Asparagus is a vegetable native to Europe, dating back to the days of ancient Rome. It is a member of the lily family, with erect stems and small scalelike leaves. The best time to buy it is around April. The name of the plant derives from the early Persian custom of eating the delicious early spears or *asparaj* (meaning "sprout"). The early, young, slender shoots are the best for juicing. The older the spears, the less delicate the flavor and the more fibrous the texture.

Asparagus used for juicing should be as fresh as possible, as the flavor dissipates quickly. The asparagus stalk will break at its freshest point. After breaking, wash the stalks, removing dirt and scales. Several stalks may be juiced at one time. If they are very long, cut them in two for easier handling.

Asparagus juice is too strong to drink undiluted. Mix with other juices (carrot is excellent) in combinations to suit your taste. Herbs such as tarragon, marjoram and savory add an agreeable flavor.

Asparagus is a good source of potassium, sodium, iron, calcium, iodine, silicon, sulfur and chlorine. The juice also provides enzymatic action that helps relieve rheumatism. One cup contains 960 IU vitamin A, 116 IU vitamin B_1, 80 IU vitamin B_2 and 1,600 IU vitamin C. Five average spears make ⅓ cup of juice. Drink the juice within 24 hours.

AVOCADOS The avocado, native to Mexico and Latin America, is now grown in Florida and California. It has an uncommonly high protein and oil content for a fruit. The fruit consists of a nut surrounded by rich, delicious flesh, which in turn is covered by green skin. The avocado ripens at room temperature. When ripe, the flesh will be soft and the skin will give slightly to the touch.

Avocados come in many varieties, shapes and sizes. The Florida crop, which is the best tasting, is available from February to late spring; the California crop is available during the fall months.

Avocados should be blended, not juiced.

BANANAS The banana is a fruit picked while not fully ripe. It makes a long journey from Central America to the consumer, during which time it is allowed to ripen. It travels well: neither the appearance nor the flavor is damaged in any way.

Buy plump bananas that are green at the top and yellow in the middle and allow them to ripen at room temperature. The indication of ripeness is the development of brown speckles. Fully ripe bananas are easily digestible in juice form, while unripened bananas are not. Bananas must be blended, not juiced. Remove the peel first.

Bananas contain a good supply of potassium as well as 190 IU vitamin A and 10 IU vitamin C.

BEETS In ancient days, the beet root (today an important food source) was considered a medicine, while the beet top was used as a vegetable.

Fresh beets are available in leafy bunches. There are two principal types of garden beets: the "early" type, which grow in cool weather and have a sweet flavor, and the "late" beets, which are planted in early summer and grow when the weather is warm. Some early varieties are Egyptian and Early Wonder; some late varieties are Detroit Dark Red and Winter Keeper. Any variety of beet can be juiced. Choose young tender beets with small firm roots and reddish-green or green tops. The red-fleshed beets generally have better flavor than the yellow ones.

For juicing, cut off the very top of the root in order to remove any hidden dirt and grit, wash the beets with cold water and cut into sections. Beet juice is high in calcium, sodium, potassium and chlorine. One cup contains 140 IU vitamin A, 48 IU vitamin B_1, 25 IU vitamin B_2 and 400 IU vitamin C. One medium-sized beet makes ¼ cup of juice. Beets aid greatly in building the blood cells. Drinking beet juice alone can, and usually does, cause a natural and dizzying high. This is due to the cleansing effect on the liver. It may be mixed with other juices to dilute its sometimes overpowering strength. Dill, ginger, thyme, allspice, chervil or cloves will spice up beet juice. Do not keep beet juice for more than 24 hours.

Beet tops can also be juiced and are especially nutritious, being very high in potassium, calcium, phosphorus, iron and sodium. One cup contains 20,000 IU vitamin A, 30 IU vitamin B_1, 75 IU vitamin B_2 and 75 IU vitamin C.

BLACKBERRIES The blackberry is a member of the same family as the raspberry. The hundreds of species of this fruit can be divided into two general categories: one kind, also known as a dewberry, grows as a trailing vine (the boysenberry is a California-grown type of dewberry); the other kind grows upright and has a stronger flavor than the dewberry. Blackberries are picked when fully ripe. They ship well and retain their freshness until they reach the consumer. Ripe berries are black. A red color indicates immaturity.

Keep blackberries cool and dry. Wash with cold water and remove stems (as well as bad berries) before either juicing or blending. The flavor of this fruit runs from sweet to bittersweet. The juice from some varieties of blackberry will be very thick and can be diluted with cold water if desired.

Blackberries are high in calcium, phosphorus, iron, sodium, potassium and sulfur. One cup contains 150 IU vitamin A, 21 IU vitamin B_1, 7 IU vitamin B_2 and 160 IU vitamin C.

BLUEBERRIES Also known as the cockatoo bush, the blueberry shrub is extensively grown in all parts of the world. The season for blueberries runs from June to August. The huckleberry, which is so dark that it is often thought to be black, is a particularly delicious blueberry.

When buying blueberries, look for plump fruits that are uniform in size and color. The waxy appearance is the result of a natural protective coat. This fruit does not store well. But, if necessary, it can be kept for short periods in the refrigerator.

Blueberry juice has a sweet flavor. Stems must be removed before either juicing or blending. The fruit is high in potassium, calcium, phosphorus, iron and sodium. One cup contains 150 IU vitamin A, 21 IU vitamin B_1, 7 IU vitamin B_2 and 160 IU vitamin C.

BROCCOLI Broccoli is a variety of cabbage and thus also related to cauliflower and Brussels sprouts. There are two kinds: the heading type, which resembles the cauliflower, and the sprouting type, which consists of a main stalk with a central cluster of small green flower buds at the end. The freshness of the vegetable depends on picking and using these buds before they open. The leaves can also be used, but they are not as delicious as the branch and buds.

Fresh broccoli, grown mostly in California, is available year-round. When buying broccoli, make sure the flower head is dark-green and that the buds on the stalks are tightly closed. Do not buy any with open yellow blossoms. Wash with cold water before juicing. A bit of thyme added to the juice gives zest to the taste.

Broccoli is high in potassium and also has a good deal of calcium, phosphorus, iron and sodium. One cup contains 8,000 IU vitamin A, 45 IU vitamin B_1, 150 IU vitamin B_2 and 1,600 IU vitamin C.

BRUSSELS SPROUTS The Brussels sprout, another member of the cabbage family, has sprouts, or buds, about the size of small walnuts, growing thickly around the stem. These sprouts are the edible and juicing part of the vegetable and are somewhat similar in tenderness and flavor to broccoli and cauliflower. The vegetable is in season from September to December. At any other time of year, fresh sprouts are not available.

Buy Brussels sprouts only when the small buds are bright-green, firm and unwrinkled. The juice is too strong to drink undiluted. Combine with carrot, lettuce or celery juice. Add some basil to the juice for a mildly peppery taste.

Brussels sprouts should be washed in cold water before juicing. They are high in potassium, along with iron, iodine, sulfur, calcium, phosphorus and sodium. One cup contains 1,100 IU vitamin A, 5 IU vitamin B_1 and 1,800 IU vitamin C. The juice is helpful to the digestive system.

CABBAGE The thousands of varieties of cabbage are among the most nutritious vegetables, and more cabbage is eaten than any other vegetable except the potato. In this country, cabbage heads range in color from green to red to white. The head can be either round or flat, the leaves either smooth or wrinkled. The varieties (which are almost endless) include bok choy, a very crisp leafy vegetable, white or green in color, with thick rounded stalks and dark-green blades, and Chinese cabbage (or celery cabbage), with broad-ribbed green to white leaves and a sharp taste.

With any variety of cabbage, make sure it is firm to the touch, fresh and crisp, with unblemished and unwilted leaves. Beware of extremes of white and green. The first means overripeness, the second, immaturity.

For juicing, wash well in cold water and cut into chunks. Cabbage juice is high in sulfur, chlorine and iodine, and also contains calcium and sodium. One cup provides 100 IU vitamin A, 50 IU vitamin B_1, 30 IU vitamin B_2 and 3,000 IU vitamin C. Two average cabbage leaves produce about one ounce (three tablespoons) of juice. A little mint spruces up the taste of the juice. Cabbage juice has great cleansing properties and helps to relieve constipation.

CANTALOUPES   This is a hard-rind variety of the muskmelon, with a gray-green ridged skin which ripens into yellow. The two most popular varieties have deep-orange flesh and light-green flesh.

Look for cantaloupes that have a smooth green indentation at the skin end. The fruits should be picked when immature and ripened at room temperature. When they are ripe, they give off a sweet aroma. If there is no sign of a stem, it means the melon was allowed to ripen on the vine. If the melon yields to a slight touch, it is already ripe, possibly overripe, and should be avoided. It should be completely firm. After it is ripened, the melon should be refrigerated.

For juicing, cut the melons up and feed the small sections into the juicer. For blending, scoop the pulp out of the hard rind and discard the rind.

Cantaloupes are high in potassium and also contain 3,400 IU vitamin A.

CARROTS   Originating in Europe and western Asia, the carrot is a member of the same family as hemlock, the deadly poison. The main nutritional value of carrots is the orange-yellow pigment known as carotene, an element that turns into vitamin A when used by the intestinal cells. Carotene is absent in other root vegetables such as turnips and parsnips, so carrots are all the more important to a daily diet. The highest concentration of carotene is found in varieties with bright golden-orange flesh.

Carrots, available year-round, are not expensive. The best ones for juicing are firm, plump, crisp and richly colored when purchased; avoid warm or wilted carrots. Cut off the tops to eliminate dirt. Wash well with cold water and scrub with a vegetable brush. Feed into the juicer without peeling or cutting into pieces. Cut into lengthwise pieces only if necessary to fit into the juicer.

Carrots are the single most valuable vegetable for juicing because they provide a sweet-tasting base for highly concentrated, bitter green vegetables. There are endless combinations that are both tasty and healthful. The favorites involve celery, spinach, beets, endive, parsley and lettuce.

The juice of the carrot increases vitality and vigor, helps improve appetite, aids digestion, eliminates mucus, aids the eyes and helps to maintain the bone structure, including teeth. Three large carrots provide one cup of juice. Four pounds of carrots make a quart of juice. Drink the juice within 24 hours, as it will not keep. For flavor add allspice, ground caraway, fennel, ginger, mace, nutmeg or thyme.

Carrots are high in potassium, iron, magnesium, sodium, silicon, iodine, sulfur, chlorine, phosphorus and calcium. One cup contains 2,700 IU vitamin A, 32 IU vitamin B_1, 32 IU vitamin B_2 and 160 IU vitamin C.

CAULIFLOWER The cauliflower plant has oddly formed heads, rolled curds, compacted flowers and upper stems. The curds should be large and closed, smooth and white. Avoid soft spots, which indicate staleness. Also avoid any type with very small leaves, for these will push their way through the head and separate the curd. Fresh cauliflower is available throughout the year. For juicing, use only very firm heads with no discoloration. The foliage should be a rich green, never yellowed. Flavor with ground caraway, dill, basil or nutmeg, if desired.

Cauliflower is high in calcium and potassium.

CELERY Celery is one vegetable every part of which may be used for juicing. It is available throughout the year. Select the green variety rather than the bleached and make sure it is fresh and crisp and has no brown spots.

Store celery as near 32° as possible. The stalks should be kept in a plastic bag during storage as they deteriorate when exposed to air.

For juicing, celery should be cool and crisp. Do not use wilted or warm celery. Wash well with cold water and feed the stalks into the juicer whole with the leaves intact. Do not keep celery juice for more than 24 hours.

Two large celery stalks with leaves make ⅓ cup of juice. Five celery stalks with leaves make one cup of juice. Celery is high in sodium chloride. It is the best natural food for counteracting the effects of extreme heat. Combined with carrot, it has a salutary effect on the nervous system. It is also high in magnesium and iron and contains potassium, calcium and sulfur. One 7-inch stalk provides 500 IU vitamin A, 5 IU vitamin B_1, 5 IU vitamin B_2, 50 IU vitamin C and vitamin E.

If taken alone, the juice can be spruced up with herbs such as chervil and marjoram.

Celeriac is a variety of celery with a large root rather than stalks and foliage. The flavor is bitter but can be sweetened by adding apple or carrot juice. Always use some of the leaves of the stalk when juicing.

CHARD   Swiss chard is a variety of the beet family with bright yellow-green leaves and thick stalks. It is usually available in the fall.

Chard contains calcium, iodine and iron, and is very high in potassium. One cup contains 20,000 IU vitamin A, 30 IU vitamin B_1, 75 IU vitamin B_2 and 1,120 IU vitamin C.

CHERRIES   Cherry trees have been providing sweet, sour and hybrid berries for centuries. Indeed, cherry pits have even been found in Stone Age caves, indicating the primitive beginnings of man's interest in the fruit, which is a member of the drupe family. Drupes are fruits that contain a single seed inside a hard stone, like the apricot.

Two distinct varieties of cherry are available—sweet and sour. Sweet cherries are used for eating and drinking, sour cherries for preserving and baking.

The most common sweet cherry is the Bing, a large heart-shaped fruit that is deep-maroon to black in color. A smaller and slightly darker variety is the Schmidt. The Bing is grown on the west coast and the Schmidt on the east coast. Their season lasts from May to August.

Choose fresh cherries that are firm, plump and brightly colored. Remove the pits before either juicing or blending. Wash with cold water and remove stems. The extracted juice of the cherry is strong and can be diluted if desired. It can also be refrigerated or frozen.

Bing cherries are high in calcium, phosphorus, iron, sodium and potassium. One cup contains 160 IU vitamin A, 20 IU vitamin B_1 and 460 IU vitamin C.

COCONUTS   The coconut grows on a palm tree. It consists of an outer husk and a large nut containing the thick edible meat and the fluid called coconut milk. The husk is usually removed before the coconut reaches the consumer. The outside skin of the nut is green until it reaches maturity.

Coconut milk is not as nutritious as the juiced raw coconut (which also contains the milk). The brown husk must be removed before juicing or blending. Coconut is high in potassium, chlorine, phosphorus, sodium, sulfur, calcium, magnesium and iron. One cup contains 16 IU vitamin B_1, 80 IU vitamin B_2 and 160 IU vitamin C.

COLLARD LEAVES   An important vegetable in the South, the collard is a non-heading variety of the cabbage family. Collard leaves are picked when young and tender and have a very strong flavor. When juicing, use only small amounts as a flavor enhancer for other juices.

Collard leaves are high in iron, potassium and chlorine.

One cup contains 10,000 IU vitamin A, 100 IU vitamin B_1, 200 IU vitamin B_2 and 10,000 IU vitamin C.

CRANBERRIES First found growing wild by the Pilgrims, the cranberry bush has slender stems and evergreen leaves with small, bright-red berries that ripen in early fall. Select berries with bright color and glossy skins. Raw cranberry juice is not very good to drink undiluted, as the flavor is acidic. It is best mixed with a generous amount of apple juice. Feed the berries into the juicer by the handful. They may also be blended.

Cranberries are high in calcium, sulfur and potassium. One cup contains 70 IU vitamin A and 400 IU vitamin C.

CUCUMBERS The cucumber is a member of the squash family. Although they are low in vitamins, cucumbers have a high mineral content and are known as an excellent diuretic.

Buy cucumbers that are firm to the touch. It is best to peel the skin before blending because most cucumbers in markets have a waxy artificial covering. For juicing, use fresh unwilted cucumbers, scrub them well, cut off ends and cut into sections to fit the throat. Mix with other juices, if desired. Do not keep over 24 hours.

One medium-sized cucumber makes about ¾ cup of juice. Cucumbers are high in silicon and sulfur, which promotes hair growth, and contain potassium, iron, magnesium and chlorine. One large cucumber contains 20 IU vitamin A, 110 IU vitamin B_1, 2 IU vitamin B_2 and 720 IU vitamin C. Herbs such as basil, mint and borage can be added to taste.

DANDELION GREENS A member of the daisy family, the dandelion is found in abundance as a weed in meadows. While the plant is usually considered a nuisance, it is actually of great value due to the vitamin content of the root.

The greens are available in big bunches during the early spring months. Choose the youngest, which are most tender. The older they get, the more fibrous they become. The juice is bitter and should be combined with a sweeter vegetable. It is rich in magnesium, high in potassium, calcium, silicon and iron. One cup contains 18,000 IU vitamin A, 36 IU vitamin B_1, 150 IU vitamin B_2 and 400 IU vitamin C. Dandelion-greens juice normalizes the alkalinity of the body's system. Use both leaves and roots. Combine with the juice of carrots and turnip leaves for a combination to strengthen the teeth.

DATES The date is the oblong fleshy fruit of the date palm, which is grown in California and Arizona. Look for plump shiny fruits with a waxy, but not sticky, surface. Dates have a very high sugar content and contain significant amounts of calcium, phosphorus and potassium. They are a relatively weak source of vitamins A, B and C.

ELDERBERRIES The elderberry is a member of the honeysuckle family. Elderberries have a sharp flavor and are considered a cure for insomnia. They may be either juiced or blended.

FENNEL There are two types of fennel. One is an herb and is not used for juicing. The Florence fennel variety comes from the same family as the carrot, the parsnip and parsley. It is sweeter than the first type and is used for juicing. The stalks have a bulblike appearance and a sweet aromatic flavor reminiscent of anise. In texture and appearance it resembles celery.

Fennel juice mixes well with carrot and beet. It is high in potassium and iron and also contains calcium and phosphorus. One cup has 1,062 IU vitamin C.

FIGS The fig is a small fruit which contains a seedy pulp with a sweet flavor. Fresh figs, which are available in September, constitute only about one quarter of all figs sold. Due to their perishability, most figs are dried. When buying fresh figs, look for fruits that are soft to the touch and have bright colors ranging from green to deep purple. Figs are a good source of calcium, phosphorus and potassium. They also contain amounts of vitamins A, B and C.

GARLIC Garlic grows in bulbs divided into about ten sections called cloves. The color can be white, purple or rose.

Garlic bulbs are always sold in a dry state. Clean by removing the outer loose parts of the sheath and trimming the roots close to the base. Store like an onion; unpeeled cloves will keep for many months.

NEVER USE GARLIC IN A JUICE EXTRACTOR! Due to its extreme potency, garlic's flavor will never wash out, and every juice thereafter will have a garlic taste. When garlic is required, use a garlic press and add the garlic juice after the vegetable or fruit juice has been separately extracted. The odor transfers easily to the hands during peeling. If this happens, scrub your hands with salt and then wash with soap and water; the offensive odor will be removed.

Garlic supplies phosphorus, iodine, calcium and fluorine and is high in potassium. One clove contains 20 IU vitamin C. The mustard oils in garlic are considered an excellent cleansing agent.

GOOSEBERRIES The gooseberry is a member of the rose family. The berry is a juicy bush fruit that is highly favored in England and available in this country in smaller, less appetizing varieties. The pale-green berry has a unique tart flavor. It can be juiced or blended.

Gooseberries have low quantities of calcium, sodium, sulfur and potassium. One cup contains 760 IU vitamin A, 56 IU vitamin B_1 and 680 IU vitamin C.

GRAPEFRUITS Grapefruits, unlike many other fruits, are picked ripe. The best ones are heavy for their size, firm and thin-skinned. Puffy-looking fruits have thick skins and are usually low in juice. The fruit should be somewhat flattened at the poles. Ripeness is important, as grapefruits contain an element called naringin that supplies the bitterness and is reduced as the fruit ripens and the flavor is balanced by fruit sugar and citric acid. Skin blemishes have no effect on quality or flavor. The best buying season for grapefruits is from mid-December to mid-May.

Grapefruits can be run through a juice extractor, in which case they must be washed and cut into sections first. However, the preferred method is the old-fashioned citrus juicer or crusher. Do not strain the fresh juice or some of the nutritive elements will be lost. The concentrated juice can be diluted with hot or cold water. It is good for blending with sharp vegetable juices. Used fresh, it has an alkalizing effect in the body.

One grapefruit makes about ¾ cup of juice. It is high in potassium, calcium and phosphorus. One cup contains 45 IU vitamin B_1, 20 IU vitamin B_2 and 2,000 IU vitamin C.

GRAPES No other fruit has as many flavors as the grape. Although grapes are grown all over the country, the best varieties for juicing are cultivated in California. Some California varieties are Black Zinfandel, Aliente, Red Flame and Tokay. Eastern grapes include Concord and Niagara. The Concord grape, one of the commercial favorites, is actually not one of the best grapes for juicing purposes.

There are certain qualities to look for when buying any kind of grapes. The color should be rich and the fruit should be plump with a waxy feel and no evidence of leakage. Shake the bunch. If they come loose easily, the grapes have been stored too long and are no longer fresh.

White seedless grapes give the most juice. For juicing and blending, wash the grapes in cold water and detach from stems, carefully removing any bad grapes. If juicing, feed by the handful.

Grape seeds give a slightly tart flavor to the juice. To avoid this, use the seedless varieties, or put the grape juice in a glass jar and leave it in the refrigerator for a day. A residue, which can be removed, will rise to the top, leaving the juice clean and free of any tartness. Grape juice stores well in the refrigerator for up to several weeks and can also be frozen.

Grapes are high in sulfur, iron, calcium, potassium and magnesium. One cup contains vitamin A, 15 IU vitamin B_1, 60 IU vitamin B_2 and 60 IU vitamin C.

HONEYDEW MELONS   Honeydew, a member of the muskmelon family, is a winter melon with a smooth skin. The pale-green to white flesh is sweet and tasty. Look for melons that weigh about five to six pounds and are six inches or so in diameter. To test for ripeness, squeeze the blossom end, which should yield to the touch. Also check for aroma.

Honeydew can be juiced or blended. When juicing, chill the melons before using, cut into sections and feed into the juicer.

JERUSALEM ARTICHOKES   This vegetable is not from Jerusalem nor is it technically an artichoke. It is actually a member of the daisy family. It has a potato-like tuber about two inches long, a sweet nutlike taste, and contains a great deal of water. There are two types: one is long with red skin; the other is round, knobby and white. While its food value is low, it is completely starchless, storing its carbohydrates in the form of inulin rather than starch, and its sugar as levulose.

Jerusalem artichokes are available in late winter. The

tubers should be firm, the skin unwrinkled. The average size is about that of a man's fist.

To juice, wash well in cold water and scrape the tubers. Cut into sections and juice. Mix with other juices if desired and do not keep more than 24 hours. The tubers are high in calcium, phosphorus and iron. One medium Jerusalem artichoke contains 46 IU vitamin B_1 and 200 IU vitamin B_2.

KALE Kale is a non-heading cabbage variety with finely cut loose leaves of diverse forms and a color range from green to brownish purple. The best leaves for juicing are green. The younger leaves have the most delicate flavor, but unfortunately the markets usually sell only the older ones.

Buy kale that is firm and not yellowed. Use the greens as soon as purchased, if possible. Tear off the leaves and discard the stalks. Wash the leaves in cold water, and juice.

Kale leaves are rich in iron, phosphorus, sulfur, potassium and calcium. One cup contains 10,000 IU vitamin A, 24 IU vitamin B_1, 400 IU vitamin B_2 and 1,440 IU vitamin C.

KELP (SEAWEED) Kelp is a useful dietary supplement. The large leaves found floating on the surface of the ocean are crushed, dried, ground and used in a powdered state. Kelp provides trace minerals that cannot be found anywhere else. The powder (or granulated form) can be added to vegetable juices. It is an excellent source of iodine.

KOHLRABI This cabbage variety is often mistaken for a turnip growing on a cabbage root. Both the leaves, which are eaten as greens, and the roots are used for juicing. Buy young, small stems, no more than two inches thick. The flavor is somewhat like that of a delicate turnip.

LEEKS The leek, a member of the lily family, is a biennial herb related to the onion and to garlic. Leeks resemble scallions and are about one foot long, with stems up to 3 inches thick.

Both the pungent leaves and the thick stalks can be juiced. Although leek juice is milder than onion juice, only drops at a time should be combined with other juices until desired taste is achieved.

Before juicing, wash with cold water to remove dirt. Sometimes the underground stalks have to be split apart lengthwise to get at the grit. Leeks contain iron, potassium, sulfur, phosphorus and calcium. One cup provides 199 IU vitamin A, 56 IU vitamin B_1 and 980 IU vitamin C.

LEMONS American lemons taste acidic because they are picked when green and allowed to ripen off the tree. In Europe, where lemons are ripened on the tree, the flavor is much sweeter.

Buy plump, heavy lemons with clean unblemished skin, insuring that juiciness is intact. Lemons can be blended or juiced in an extractor or a citrus squeezer. The last is preferable. If the juice extractor is used, wash the lemon in cold water and cut into sections to fit into the feeder. The peels are also juiced for a more concentrated flavor.

Lemons provide calcium, magnesium and potassium. One medium lemon supplies 20 IU vitamin B_1 and 1,100 IU vitamin C. The lemon is the richest food in the bioflavanoids that regulate the body temperature. The juice, taken in small quantities, is an effective antacid.

LETTUCE Four basic types of lettuce are used domestically: (1) loose-leaf, non-heading, (2) the butterheads, such as Boston lettuce, which have a soft buttery head, yellow toward the center, with dark outer leaves, (3) cos, or romaine, forming a long head with oblong leaves, and (4) the cabbage heads, such as iceberg lettuce, which are the most common variety, since they ship best. In addition to regular lettuce varieties, leafy green relatives such as leafy endive, chicory and escarole are also useful for juicing.

Lettuce leaves are actually enlarged root leaves. They should be crisp and full and show no signs of blemishes or wilting. Lettuce must be washed when purchased, then dried. If left wet, it will quickly wilt and lose much of its flavor.

Romaine lettuce grows in heights of up to two feet. The outer leaves are dark-green; the leaves closer to the center turn a lighter shade. Romaine has a sharper taste than other varieties of lettuce.

Five leaves of romaine make about $\frac{1}{4}$ cup of juice, which is high in potassium and sodium. One average head contains 13,000 IU vitamin A, 40 IU vitamin B_1, 100 IU vitamin B_2 and 200 IU vitamin C.

Iceberg lettuce is best mixed with carrot juice, which improves the somewhat bitter flavor, adds vitamin A and helps to maintain the calcium content of the lettuce juice. Three average leaves supply $\frac{1}{4}$ cup of juice. Iceberg lettuce contains calcium, potassium, sulfur, silicon and phosphorus. It is high in iron and magnesium. One head provides 600 IU vitamin A, 8 IU vitamin B_1, 68 IU vitamin B_2, 360 IU vitamin C, and vitamin E. Chervil, coriander, dill, rosemary, sage or thyme will add flavor.

Leafy endive is a nutritious salad plant, highly valued for its mineral content. It differs from lettuce in its slightly more bitter flavor. The bitterness is reduced by a commercial blanching process in which, after picking, the outer leaves are tied together to enclose the heart, which turns white and develops a delicious taste.

Although endive can be kept in the refrigerator for about a week, it is best purchased and juiced fresh. Avoid wilted or discolored leaves.

Belgian endives are imported bleached centers of the

plant. These hearts are strictly specialty items. They can be quite expensive. They should be firm, pale-yellow to white in color and free from spots.

For juicing purposes, use both the outer green leaves and the hearts. The bitter flavor is best blended with carrot, celery and parsley. One handful of endive makes ¼ cup of endive juice. Endive is high in potassium, fluorine, sulfur and manganese. One 6-inch stalk contains 1,900 IU vitamin A, 23 IU vitamin B_1, 45 IU vitamin B_2 and 135 IU vitamin C. Mixed with carrot and celery, it helps alleviate hay fever and also aids the eyes.

Open curled-leaf bunches of chicory are often mistakenly sold in this country as endive. Chicory is also confused with escarole. Chicory has a very bitter-flavored curly leaf which makes an interesting addition to a salad and also a good addition to a vegetable drink. The leaves can range in color from bleached white to yellow, green and even red. Clean thoroughly before juicing.

Escarole is scientifically the same vegetable as leafy endive, the only difference being in the broadness of the leaves. Bunches of escarole consist of large, broad leaves with curly edges. The bunch is usually somewhat flattened in shape and has a yellowish center.

Escarole is very bitter and must be mixed with other juices. Rinse and clean thoroughly before juicing.

LIMES The lime is a greenish-yellow globular fruit with a very acid pulp. It is similar to the lemon in acidity but less tart. The majority of limes sold in this country are imported from either the Middle East or the South Pacific.

Buy limes that are bright-green. Juice in a citrus squeezer. Limes contain calcium, potassium and phosphorus. One medium lime provides 1,600 IU vitamin C.

MUSTARD GREENS Mustard greens are the young leaves of the mustard plant. The leaves of the white variety are milder than those of the black. Use six- to twelve-inch leaves and always mix with other juices. Mustard oils are too potent when taken alone in any quantity.

Mustard greens are high in sulfur, potassium, phosphorus, iron, magnesium and silicon. One pound supplies 92,000 IU vitamin A, 207 IU vitamin B_1, 675 IU vitamin B_2 and 6,500 IU vitamin C.

NECTARINES Nectarines are a smooth-skinned variation of the peach grown on both the west coast and in Florida. The flesh of the nectarine is firmer and more aromatic than that of the peach. Most of the major varieties are clingstone.

Buy nectarines that have no trace of green at the stem and allow them to ripen at room temperature. When ripe, they will yield slightly to pressure. Refrigerate after ripening. Remove the pit and stems before juicing. If blending, peel them. Nectarines contain iron, phosphorus and sodium and are high in potassium. One pound contains 48,000 IU vitamin A and 480 IU vitamin C.

ONIONS Many varieties of onion are available in this country, ranging from the yellow to the globular-rooted Bermuda type to the sweet, red Italian to the tiny white onions. The bulbous part of the plant is the edible portion, consisting of easily separated layers with a strong, sharp smell and taste, which is due to an oil rich in sulfur. Store in refrigerator, and place in plastic bags if cut.

Juice onion in a garlic press. NEVER JUICE THROUGH A JUICE EXTRACTOR. As with garlic, the taste can never be washed away. Use sparingly only to flavor other juices.

Onions are high in sulfur, potassium, phosphorus, calcium, chlorine, magnesium, iron and iodine. One medium onion contains 500 IU vitamin A, 24 IU vitamin B_1, 60 IU vitamin B_2 and 75 IU vitamin C.

The scallion is a milder member of the onion family

with small, nut-sized bulbs. Both the green and white parts
of the scallion may be juiced, but only in a garlic press,
not in a juice extractor.

ORANGES The orange is technically a berry with a
reddish-yellow leathery, aromatic rind. It is grown domestically in California and Florida and is available the
year round. As a rule, the California varieties are deeper
orange, have thicker skins and give less juice than the
Florida oranges. The best Florida varieties are the Parson
Brown, the Pineapple orange and the Temple orange.
Most California oranges are of the navel variety, a seedless fruit with good flavor.

Good Florida oranges are small, heavy and thin-
skinned. Most California varieties have thicker skins.
Choose small oranges; they usually provide more juice
and flavor than the large sizes (and cost less). Juice in a
citrus squeezer. If desired, oranges can be juiced in an
extractor, which will provide an extremely concentrated
taste, much stronger than what we are used to. To juice
in the extractor, wash the orange in cold water and cut
into sections to fit the feeding throat. Use all parts of the
peel for high concentration. Drink the juice within ten
minutes. Peeled oranges can also be blended.

Orange juice contains magnesium, sulfur and a very
high amount of calcium and phosphorus. One cup contains 625 IU vitamin A, 62 IU vitamin B_1, 15 IU vitamin
B_2 and 825 IU vitamin C. Orange juice assists in bone
formation. It is very high in fruit sugar and is a good body
cleanser.

PAPAYA In their natural habitat in the tropics papayas
are called "melons that grow on trees." The oblong fruit
weighs from two to twenty pounds and is yellow to orange
with a soft texture and black seeds in the middle (much
like a cantaloupe). The flavor compares with that of the
peach or the cantaloupe.

Papaya contains papain, which is excellent for the digestive system. The greenish fruit should be used because it contains more active enzymes than the ripe fruit. Also, choose round rather than oblong papayas. Papayas are extremely perishable, do not store well and therefore are not widely available in this country. For this reason, papayas often reach us in a milky juice form, which has become a popular commercial item.

However, if you are lucky enough to come across a fresh papaya, it may be either juiced or blended. Peel before juicing, and also remove seeds before blending. The papaya contains potassium and silicon. Eight ounces contain 5,750 IU vitamin A, 58 IU vitamin B_1, 1,380 IU vitamin B_2 and 1,970 IU vitamin C.

PARSLEY Parsley is a member of the carrot family. There are a number of varieties, all of which have a delicious flavor and aroma and are excellent as additives to other vegetable juices.

Parsley juice is too potent to drink undiluted. Never use more than one or two ounces at a time. Blend with carrots, celery or lettuce. Eight sprigs of parsley will produce about one ounce (three tablespoons) of juice.

Parsley is rich in potassium, calcium, sodium, magnesium, phosphorus, sulfur, chlorine and iron. One tablespoon provides 1,000 IU vitamin A, and vitamin B_1, vitamin B_2 and vitamin C. Blended parsley juice is said to be helpful in alleviating menstrual cramps and it aids in oxygen metabolism.

PARSNIPS The parsnip is a member of the carrot family with a delicate and unique flavor and the texture of a soft carrot. Parsnips are the least used of all the root vegetables. Store parsnips in a dark place, free of drafts, as too much air will bring out flavor that will be too strong for a juice. Never use the wild variety of parsnip, as it contains poisonous elements. Cut off the ends before juicing. Dill or marjoram can be added to spice up the flavor.

Parsnips are rich in potassium, phosphorus, sulfur, chlorine and calcium. One cup contains 100 IU vitamin B and 1,035 IU vitamin C.

PEACHES   Peaches have a single seed enclosed in a hard outer casing. The pulp is yellow to white and the skin is smooth and downy. The white varieties have the most delicate flavor. Peaches should ripen on the tree. Their season runs from July through September. As they do not keep well after picking, they should be purchased during this period. The test for ripeness is an increasing yield when squeezed. A ripe peach will be tender. Remove the seed and stems before juicing. For blending, also remove the skin.

Peaches contain magnesium, sulfur and potassium. One medium peach contains 900 IU vitamin A, 28 IU vitamin B_1 and 70 IU vitamin C.

PEARS   The soft, juicy pear supplies very little protein and fat. Some favorite varieties are Bartlett, Gorham, Clapp Favorite, Tyson and Winter Nelis.

Buy pears that are firm, plump and free of signs of bruising and cuts on the skin. Remove the stems before juicing. For blending, peel, core and remove stems. Pears are high in iron, magnesium and potassium. One medium pear contains 2,000 IU vitamin A, 275 IU vitamin B_1, 172 IU vitamin B_2 and 900 IU vitamin C.

PEPPERS   Peppers, which are both green and red, are large, bell-shaped vegetables available throughout the year. They belong to the same family as the potato, the tomato and the eggplant.

Pick firm peppers with no wrinkles and store in the refrigerator. Discard the inner pulp and seeds before juicing, as they have a somewhat sour flavor. Wash with cold water and cut into sections to fit the juicer feeder. Do not keep the juice over 24 hours. One small pepper makes about ½ cup of juice. Green peppers are high in silicon, which is good for the hair and nails. One medium pepper contains 1,500 IU vitamin A, 67 IU vitamin B_1, 40 IU vitamin B_2 and 2,000 IU vitamin C.

PINEAPPLES A native of Hawaii, the pineapple is a solid mass of succulent fleshy fruit surrounded by a tough outer skin and crowned with small leaves. Among the varieties are Red Spanish (yellow to orange, with white flesh), which is the mainstay of the United States market, and Cayenne (smoother-edged leaves, yellow to green when ripe).

If a pineapple is not ripe when purchased, allow it to stand at room temperature until it is. At this time it will give off a delightful fragrance. The true test of the freshness of a pineapple is the aroma. Another test is that, when ripe, the quilted flesh gives under the skin and the leaves readily fall off when pulled. Only ripe pineapples should be juiced or blended. Remove the outside shell, leaving the inside intact. Cut the pineapple into sections to feed to the juicer. Do this over a bowl, as valuable juice will otherwise be lost. Pineapple juice stores well and can be kept under refrigeration for quite a few days.

Pineapple juice, which is quite thick, is known as an excellent dessert drink, as it contains a valuable enzyme which aids in the digestive process. It is rich in potassium, chlorine, sodium, phosphorus, magnesium, sulfur, calcium, iron and iodine. One cup contains 200 IU vitamin A, 70 IU vitamin B_1, 20 IU vitamin B_2 and 700 IU vitamin C.

PLUMS There are four major varieties of plum: American, Damson, European and Japanese, with colors rang-

ing from dark-red to royal-purple to golden. The red
Japanese plums are the best for juicing. These are juiced
when ripe to ensure the availability of enough natural
sugar to counteract the normal acidity.

Buy full, plump plums. Ripe plums have a softening
at the tip as well as a delightful aroma. The firmness
should be midway between soft and hard. Remove the
seed before juicing. Remove both the seed and the skin
before blending. Plums are rich in iron, calcium, magnesium and potassium. One medium plum contains 180
IU vitamin A, 12 IU vitamin B_1, 5 IU vitamin B_2 and
50 IU vitamin C.

POMEGRANATES The pomegranate is about the size
of an orange. It contains multiple seeds in a reddish pulp
and is surrounded by a thick rind. The pulp is sweet and
is known as a cool refresher in warm climates.

Pomegranates should be ripe, as indicated by a slight
cracking of the skin. For juicing, remove the bitter rind.
Do not remove the inner seeds. Pomegranate juice is best
diluted with other fruit drinks (although it can be taken
alone): one part pomegranate to five parts other juices.
It contains magnesium and sodium. One medium fruit
provides 450 IU vitamin C.

POTATOES The potato is probably the most popular
vegetable in the world and is a primary source of starch.
There are dozens of varieties of potato marketed in the
United States.

Buy potatoes that are firm and crisp. Store them in a
cool dark place with good ventilation. Before juicing,
check thoroughly for bruises and decayed spots. Raw potato juice contains easily digestible natural sugars. After
cooking, this turns to starch. Juice with skin intact. The
skin, however, should be removed before using in a
blender. Potatoes are high in potassium, sulfur, phos-

phorus and chlorine. One medium potato contains 80 IU vitamin A, 75 IU vitamin B_1, 40 IU vitamin B_2 and 500 IU vitamin C. One potato makes about one cup of juice. It is very palatable when taken alone. It can also be combined with other juices. It's a good idea to let the juice settle for a minute or so to allow the loose starch to go to the bottom. Pour the juice off and drink. Don't keep for more than 24 hours. Ginger, dill or oregano will add flavor.

Sweet potatoes are much higher in potassium, sulfur, phosphorus and chlorine than white potatoes. One medium sweet potato contains 7,000 IU vitamin A, 60 IU vitamin B_1, 60 IU vitamin B_2 and 800 IU vitamin C. One sweet potato makes about ¾ cup of juice.

RADISH White, black and purple as well as red radishes can be used for juice, which is extracted from the leaves and roots. Wash the radishes in cold water and cut off the tips to eliminate hidden dirt. Do not juice the stems. Radish juice should be used in combination with carrot and celery juice and should be consumed within one half hour after juicing. Seven radishes make about ¼ cup of juice. It is high in potassium, iron and magnesium as well as sodium, sulfur, chlorine and phosphorus. One cup contains vitamin A, 40 IU vitamin B_1, 20 IU vitamin B_2 and 800 IU vitamin C.

RASPBERRIES The raspberry is the most important of the bramble fruits and is considered the best tasting of all berries.

Raspberries should be juiced or blended as soon as possible, as they do not keep more than a few days. Buy plump, firm fruits, bright in color and dry on the outside. Remove the stems before juicing or blending. The raspberry has a subtle flavor and should be mixed only with juices that are also delicate. Raspberries are high in potassium, calcium, phosphorus and sulfur. One cup contains 20 IU vitamin A, 18 IU vitamin B_1 and 660 IU vitamin C.

RHUBARB   Rhubarb, a spring plant, is used as both a fruit and a vegetable. The stalks, a foot to a foot and a half long, contain juice that is very acidic, therefore limited in use. The younger stalks are the ones to buy. They should be firm, tender and red. For juicing, they should be washed in cold water, trimmed and cut into small pieces.

Combine sparingly with carrot, celery or fruit juice. Rhubarb juice contains calcium, potassium and sulfur. One cup contains 230 IU vitamin A, 18 IU vitamin B_1 and 360 IU vitamin C.

ROSE HIPS   The rose has been a culinary delight for hundreds of years. Rose hips consist of the ripe fruit of the rose and can be taken from any kind of rose. This fruit is the hard bulblike object inside the center of the rose. Pieces of this fruit are an excellent additive to fresh drinks and juices. Fresh rose hips may be obtained right from the garden. The commonly used dry rose hips are sold in tea-bag form.

SORREL   Sorrel is a perennial vegetable with large, thick red-root leaves, sour in flavor. It is available in limited supply in the spring. The varieties marketed in this country are Spinach Dock (dock is another name for sorrel), Belleville sorrel and Fresh sorrel.

Look for large rather than thick root leaves. Before juicing, wash with cold water to remove grit and dirt. Blend with other juices to relieve the sourness, which is caused by oxalic acid. Sorrel juice tastes especially good mixed with spinach juice.

Sorrel is rich in potassium, iron and magnesium. It also has substantial amounts of phosphorus, sulfur and silicon.

SPINACH Spinach is a potherb, a leafy green grown only for its foliage. The greenish, arrow-shaped leaves can be wrinkled or smooth, and vary in color from dark-green to pale-green. It is in season during spring and autumn.

Buy spinach that has wide, thick leaves. Wash with cold water to remove grit. For juicing, cut off the stems and tear the leaves into large pieces. Place these pieces in a pot of cold water and swish for a few seconds (don't soak) before juicing. Basil, nutmeg, curry or thyme will add flavor.

One handful of spinach makes about three tablespoons of juice. It is a good source of potassium, sodium, calcium, iodine, magnesium and iron. One pound contains 90,000 IU vitamin A, 207 IU vitamin B_1, 598 IU vitamin B_2 and 5,850 IU vitamin C. Spinach juice is the most vital vegetable juice for the entire digestive tract. It is extremely potent alone and best mixed with other vegetable juices such as carrot, celery and lettuce.

STRAWBERRIES The strawberry, like the raspberry, is a member of the rose family. There are thousands of varieties of strawberry in different shapes, sizes and shades of red.

Buy plump, red strawberries. Beware of white patches, which indicate the fruit has been picked unripe. Avoid poorly shaped strawberries, and buy during the peak of the season, which is May and June. The strawberry bruises easily and should be used as soon as possible. Refrigerate before use, and remove the stem endings before juicing or blending.

Strawberries contain iodine, sodium and silicon and are high in iron. One cup contains 2,900 IU vitamin C.

SUNFLOWER SEEDS The sunflower seed consists of a seed covered by green flesh, which is rich in oil, nutritious and good-tasting. This is one of the native American foods, first cultivated by American Indians, who used the seeds as a regular dietary staple. Sunflower seeds are blended.

TANGERINES   The tangerine is a variety of orange, although it is usually considered a separate fruit. Buy tangerines that are orange-red with tight skins. Juice with a citrus squeezer or, if desired, juice in an extractor or blend as with the orange.

Tangerines contain magnesium, calcium and potassium. One medium tangerine contains 280 IU vitamin A, 22 IU vitamin B_1, 7 IU vitamin B_2 and 560 IU vitamin C.

TOMATOES   Until comparatively recently the tomato was grown as an ornamental fruit, considered poisonous and not used as food.

Tomatoes must be ripe before picking. There are many varieties and colors (red, yellow, green) and many different sizes. Only red tomatoes are used for juicing. Look for medium-sized fruits that are plump and round. Cut to fit into the juicer and feed slowly. A little honey, basil, chervil or tarragon may be added after juicing.

One medium tomato makes about ⅔ cup of juice. Tomatoes contain large amounts of sodium, calcium, potassium and magnesium. They are high in amino acids. One cup contains 7,064 IU vitamin A, 60 IU vitamin B_1, 10 IU vitamin B_2 and 650 IU vitamin C.

TURNIPS   Turnips are a good-flavored root vegetable. The root comes in different sizes and shapes (flat, round, cylindrical), which all taste alike.

For juicing, use both the tubers with white or purple roots and/or the edible young leaves. Buy turnips with leaves intact and look for firmness to the touch. Wash and scrub well.

One small turnip root provides about ½ cup of juice. The turnip provides the highest percentage of calcium of all vegetables. It is high in potassium, sodium, iron, sulfur, phosphorus, magnesium and chlorine. One pound of turnips contains 45,000 IU vitamin A, 56 IU vitamin B_1, vitamin B_2, 880 IU vitamin C and vitamin E. It tastes best when mixed with coconut and celery juice. Flavor enhancers are curry and dill.

WATERCRESS Watercress, a perennial herb found submerged in streams, is a relative of the turnip and the cabbage and has a sharp flavor.

Buy firm, bright-green watercress. Juice both the stems and the leaves. Almost half the elements in watercress are acid-forming, so the juice should be blended with carrot or celery juice. A combination of carrot, spinach, small amounts of lettuce, turnip leaves and watercress is a deliciously rich drink, which is especially good for people who are underweight.

One quarter bunch of watercress makes about ⅛ cup of juice. Watercress contains phosphorus, chlorine, potassium, magnesium, iron and iodine and is very high in sulfur. One bunch provides 4,000 IU vitamin A, 56 IU vitamin B_1, vitamin B_2, 880 IU vitamin C, and vitamin E.

WATERMELON The only way to tell the quality of a watermelon is to cut it open in halves or quarters. The best melons for juicing have red flesh and dark seeds. Before juicing, remove the rind. Before blending, remove both rind and seeds.

Watermelon contains phosphorus, potassium, calcium and sodium. One half melon contains 770 IU vitamin A, 73 IU vitamin B_1, 80 IU vitamin B_2 and 1,200 IU vitamin C. One pound of watermelon makes two cups of juice.

YOGURT Yogurt is neither a fruit nor a vegetable, but it is a delicious, healthful addition to fruit and vegetable juice combinations. It is a dairy product—plain milk is injected with bacteria and heated for several hours at temperatures exceeding 100° until a sour-flavored curd is formed. Yogurt has a very high nutritional value and is considered a good way to drink milk because (1) the proteins of the milk have already been digested by the bacteria, and (2) the calcium in the milk is made more available.

🌸 VEGETABLE DRINKS

(Unless otherwise indicated, the following recipes make 1 serving.)

HEALTHFUL CARROT

8 sprigs parsley
2 carrots
1 stalk celery

Juice the parsley first, then follow with other ingredients in juice extractor. Garnish with a whole sprig of parsley.

CARROT-PARSLEY

8 sprigs parsley
3 carrots

In juice extractor juice the parsley, then the carrots. Garnish with a whole sprig of parsley.

POTASSIUM DRINK

¼ bunch parsley
1 leaf kelp
1 carrot
½ turnip

1 parsnip
½ green pepper
½ small tomato
½ potato

Juice all ingredients in juice extractor, parsley and kelp
first. Juice ½ clove of garlic in garlic press and add to
drink. Add a few drops of lemon juice.

SPINACH-BEET

1 handful spinach	Juice the spinach first, then
2 carrots	the other ingredients.
½ small beet	

TURNIP-LETTUCE

2 leaves romaine lettuce	Juice the lettuce first.
2 carrots	
½ turnip	

CARROT-MINT

3 leaves iceberg lettuce	Juice the lettuce first, then the spinach, then the
1 handful spinach	carrots. Garnish with a
2 carrots	sprig of fresh mint.

VEGETABLE-TARRAGON

2 handfuls spinach	Juice the spinach first, then
½ small tomato	the tomato, then the
2 carrots	carrots. Garnish with a pinch of ground tarragon.

CELERY-TWIST

2 red radishes or ½ white radish	Juice the radishes first, then the celery and carrots.
2 stalks celery	
2 carrots	

CARROT-RADISH

4 radishes
2 carrots

Juice the radishes first.

CELERY-LETTUCE-SPINACH

5 leaves romaine
  lettuce
2 handfuls spinach
3 stalks celery

First juice the lettuce, then the spinach, then the celery stalks.

CABBAGE COOLER

2 leaves cabbage
2 stalks celery
1½ carrots

First juice the cabbage, then the celery and carrots. Garnish with a sprig of fresh mint.

CARROT-DILL

3 leaves iceberg
  lettuce
1 stalk celery
2 carrots

First juice the lettuce, then the celery and carrots. Garnish with a pinch of dill.

CARROT-PARSNIP

1 parsnip
2 carrots

Juice the parsnip first.

VEGE-HERB

2 leaves endive
2 carrots
2 stalks celery

Juice the endive first. Garnish with a pinch of basil.

CARROT SHAKE

2 carrots
⅓ cup milk

Juice the carrots, then slowly add the milk through the opening of the extractor.

CARROT-ANISE

3 carrots
pinch ground anise
    seed

Juice the carrots, then mix in the anise seed.

CARROT-FENNEL

½ fennel root
3 carrots

Juice the fennel first.

VEGETABLE BURST

1 sprig parsley
1 handful spinach
2 carrots
2 stalks celery

First juice the parsley, then the spinach. Garnish with a whole sprig of parsley.

PARSLEY FLIP

8 sprigs parsley
1 stalk celery
½ cucumber

First juice the parsley, then add the celery and cucumber. Add a few drops of lemon juice. Mix well. Garnish with a cucumber slice.

GINGER-VEG

1 *handful spinach* 3 *stalks celery* 2 *carrots*	First juice the spinach, then the celery and carrots. Garnish with a pinch of ground ginger.

CARROT-PEPPER

½ *green pepper* 2 *carrots*	Juice the pepper first.

TURNIP FLIP

¼ *bunch watercress* 2 *carrots* ½ *turnip*	Juice the watercress first. Garnish with a whole sprig of watercress.

ASPARAGUS SPRITZ

4 *stalks asparagus* 2 *carrots*	Juice the asparagus first.

STRING BEAN COCKTAIL

1 *handful spinach* 10 *string beans* 2 *carrots*	First juice the spinach, then the string beans and carrots.

BEET TOP-CARROT

1 *small beet with a* *few of its tops* 2 *carrots*	First juice the beet tops, then the beet root and carrots.

SPINACH-DANDELION

2 sprigs dandelion
  greens
1 handful spinach
2 carrots

First juice the dandelion
greens, then the spinach,
then the carrots.

CARROT-BEET

2 carrots
1 medium beet

Garnish with a slice of
lemon.

STRING BEAN-CELERY

¼ pound string
  beans
4 stalks celery

Juice the beans first.

SPINACH-CARROT

1 handful spinach
3 carrots

Juice the spinach first.

CARROT-GINGER

2 handfuls spinach
2 carrots

Juice the spinach first.
Garnish with a pinch of
ground ginger.

CARROT-CUCUMBER-LETTUCE

3 leaves romaine
  lettuce
⅓ cucumber
2 carrots

First juice the lettuce, then
the cucumber and carrots.
Garnish with a pinch of
dill.

CARROT DANDY

1 handful dandelion
   greens
2 carrots

Juice the dandelion greens
first.

STRING BEAN DELIGHT

3 leaves iceberg
   lettuce
¼ pound string
   beans
2 carrots

First juice the lettuce,
then the beans, last the
carrots. Garnish with a
pinch of ground rosemary.

PARSNIP SURPRISE

5 sprigs watercress
1 carrot
¼ potato
1 parsnip

Juice the watercress first.
Garnish with a whole
sprig of watercress.

STRING BEAN-CARROT

¼ pound string
   beans
2 carrots

Juice the beans first.

POTATO-CRESS

3 sprigs watercress
1 stalk celery
¼ potato
2 carrots

Juice the watercress first.
Garnish with a whole
sprig of watercress.

CARAWAY-BEET DELIGHT

2 carrots
1 small beet

Garnish with a pinch of
ground caraway.

WATERCRESS STINGER

5 sprigs watercress
1 handful spinach
2 carrots
½ turnip

First juice the watercress
and spinach, then the
other ingredients. Garnish
with a whole sprig of
watercress.

CARROT-CABBAGE

3 leaves cabbage
2 carrots

Juice the cabbage first.

ROMAINE DELIGHT

3 leaves romaine
   lettuce
1½ carrots
1 small beet
½ turnip

Juice the lettuce first.

CELERY ROYALE

8 sprigs parsley
2 handfuls spinach
3 stalks celery

First juice the parsley,
then the spinach, then the
celery. Garnish with a
whole sprig of parsley.

CARROT BURST

5 sprigs parsley
1 handful spinach
1 stalk celery
2 carrots

First juice the parsley, followed by the spinach, then celery and carrots.

CARROT-TURNIP

2 carrots
½ turnip

Garnish with a pinch of dill.

CARROT-ALMOND DRINK

½ cup carrot juice
¼ cup almond
   slivers
½ cup milk

Put all ingredients in blender and mix until smooth. Garnish with a sprinkle of nutmeg. (Serves 2.)

ENDIVE DELIGHT

3 leaves endive
4 sprigs parsley
1 stalk celery
2 carrots

First juice the endive, then the parsley and celery, then the carrots.

PEPPER JUBILEE

½ green pepper
1 small beet
1 stalk celery
1 carrot

First juice the pepper, then the beet and celery, then the carrot.

ALFALFA STINGER

| 1 handful alfalfa | Juice the alfalfa first. |
| 2 carrots | Garnish with a sprig of fresh mint. |

CARROT ROYALE

1½ carrots	Juice all ingredients.
1 stalk celery	
1 medium beet	

DANDELION SPECIAL

1 handful dandelion greens	First juice the dandelion greens, then the spinach and last the celery.
1 handful spinach	
4 stalks celery	

DILL-VEG

⅓ turnip	First juice the turnip, then the cucumber and last the celery. Garnish with a pinch of dill.
⅓ cucumber	
4 stalks celery	

MINT-CABBAGE

| 4 leaves cabbage | First juice the cabbage, then the celery. Garnish with a sprig of fresh mint. |
| 4 stalks celery | |

WATERCRESS-CARROT

½ bunch watercress
2 carrots

Juice the watercress first. Garnish with a whole sprig of watercress.

CARROT-KALE

2 leaves kale
2 carrots
1 stalk celery

First juice the kale, then the other ingredients. Garnish with a pinch of ground marjoram.

CARROT-LETTUCE

3 leaves romaine
  lettuce
2 carrots

Juice the lettuce first.

VEGETABLE JUBILEE

3 sprigs parsley
2 handfuls spinach
¼ cucumber
3 stalks celery

First juice the parsley, then the spinach, followed by the cucumber and celery. Garnish with a whole sprig of parsley.

RADISH-BEET

3 leaves escarole
  radish
  scallion
  small beet
  carrots

First juice the escarole, then the radish, scallion, beet and carrots.

VEGETABLE-SAGE

½ *cucumber*
2 *carrots*

Juice the cucumber, then the carrots. Garnish with a pinch of ground sage.

❧ FRUIT DRINKS*

PEACH FUZZ

2 oranges
2 peaches
1 plum

Squeeze the oranges.
Juice the peaches and
plum. Combine juices and
mix well. Garnish with a
peach slice.

ORANGE-PINEAPPLE

2 oranges
juice from ½ lemon
⅓ cup pineapple juice
 (unsweetened)

Squeeze the oranges. Add
the other ingredients to
the orange juice and mix
well. Garnish with an
orange slice.

APPLE-GRAPE

1 McIntosh apple
½ cup grape juice
 (unsweetened)

Juice the apple and mix
with the grape juice.

* When fruit juice is called for in the following recipes, it should be
freshly squeezed, extracted or blended. However, some recipes call
for "unsweetened" fruit juice. This indicates canned or bottled
juices without preservatives which are available in health-food or
regular markets. They are used to flavor and dilute drinks which
would be too thick if the fruit were either extracted or blended.

APPLE SHAKE

½ cup apple juice
1 scoop ice cream
    (select to taste)

Put ingredients in blender
and mix until smooth.
Garnish with slices of
apple.

GRAPE O'LAY

1 cup apple juice
½ pear
½ cup grape juice
1 teaspoon chopped
    mint leaves

Put all the ingredients in
blender and whip until
smooth. Serve over
crushed ice; garnish with
whole sprigs of fresh
mint. (Serves 3.)

DATE-MILK DRINK

1 cup soybean milk,
    page 16
1 tablespoon slivered
    almonds
3 pitted dates

Mix the ingredients to-
gether in blender until
smooth. Garnish with a
dash of nutmeg.

ORANGE TEA

3 oranges
1 cup lime flower tea
juice of 1 lemon
1 cup soda water

Put the ingredients in
blender and mix until
foamy. Serve over ice.
Garnish with lime slices.
(Serves 3.)

COCONUT-ORANGE

½ cup orange juice
½ cup milk
¼ cup shredded
    coconut
¼ teaspoon powdered
    orange rind*

Mix ingredients in blender
until smooth. Garnish with
orange slices. (Serves 2.)

* Powdered fruit rinds are available in most supermarkets.

ROSY TOMATO

½ cup tomato juice
1 teaspoon lemon
    juice
½ cup rose-hip
    juice*
drop of mint extract

Blend ingredients until
smooth. Garnish with
sprigs of fresh mint.

* Rose-hip juice: For 15 minutes simmer ½ cup rose hips in 3
cups water. Strain and use juice.

MINTED APRICOT DRINK

1 cup apricot nectar
    (unsweetened)
sprig of mint, finely
    chopped
pinch ground mace

Blend ingredients. Garnish
with a whole sprig of
fresh mint.

RAISIN BURST

1 cup water
juice of ½ lemon
½ cantaloupe, cut up
1 tablespoon soft-
    ened* raisins

Put ingredients in blender
and whip until smooth.
Serve over ice. (Serves
2–3.)

* Soaked in water for 15 minutes.

FRUITED MILK

½ cup milk
¼ banana, sliced
½ cup fresh fruit
   juice (select to
   taste)
3 tablespoons
   powdered milk

Mix ingredients in blender
until smooth. Garnish
with orange slices.
(Serves 2.)

APRICOT LIFT

½ cup apricot nectar
   (unsweetened)
½ cup pineapple
   juice (unsweetened)

Whip ingredients in
blender until foamy. Gar-
nish with a sprig of fresh
mint.

APPLE-PEAR

1 pear
2 apples

First juice the pear, then
the apples. Garnish with
an apple slice.

MINTED FRUIT DRINK

½ cup fresh fruit
   (select to taste)
1½ teaspoons honey
2 drops mint extract
juice of ½ lemon
1 cup milk

Mix ingredients in blender
until smooth. Garnish with
sprigs of fresh mint.
(Serves 2.)

STRAWBERRY-DATE FIZZ

½ cup fresh straw-
  berries
1 cup crushed ice
½ cup pitted dates

Mix ingredients in blender
until slightly mushy.
Garnish with orange slices.
(Serves 2.)

APRICOT-HONEY DRINK

½ cup apricot nectar
3 tablespoons honey
½ cup milk

Mix ingredients until
smooth in blender. Garnish
with orange slices.

APPLE-GRAPEFRUIT

1 apple
1 grapefruit

First juice the apple, then
squeeze the grapefruit.
Garnish with an orange
slice.

POMEGRANATE-MELON FREEZE

½ small cantaloupe
1 pomegranate
2 cups watermelon
  chunks

First juice the cantaloupe,
then the pomegranate and
watermelon. Strain. If too
thick, water down with
orange juice. (Serves 2.)

PEACHY PINEAPPLE

1 peach
½ cup pineapple juice
    (unsweetened)
½ cup milk
1 teaspoon honey

Cut the peach into small pieces. Put ingredients into blender. Mix until smooth. (Serves 2.)

STRAWBERRY SUNSHINE

8 strawberries
2 apples

First juice the strawberries, then add the apples. Garnish with whole fresh strawberries.

RASPBERRYADE

1 pint fresh rasp-
    berries
juice of 4 lemons
1 cup water

Put ingredients in blender and mix with small amounts of honey until sweet enough. Garnish with lemon slices. (Serves 4–5.)

BANANA FLIP

½ cup sliced bananas
½ cup milk
1 teaspoon honey
½ cup pineapple
    juice
2 drops vanilla
    extract

Whip ingredients in blender until smooth. Garnish with an orange slice. (Serves 2.)

COCONUT-PINEAPPLE

½ cup pineapple
   juice
½ cup milk
¼ cup shredded
   coconut
2 teaspoons honey

Mix ingredients in blender
until smooth and foamy.
Garnish with pineapple
wedges. (Serves 2.)

APPLE-PINEAPPLE

1 apple
¾ cup pineapple juice
   (unsweetened)

Juice the apple. Mix with
pineapple juice. Garnish
with pineapple wedges.

PEACHY APPLE

1 peach
½ cup apple juice
1 teaspoon honey
½ cup crushed ice

Cut the peach into small
pieces. Put ingredients in
blender and whip until
smooth. Garnish with
apple slices. (Serves 2.)

PRUNE MILK SHAKE

1 cup milk
¼ cup prune juice
   (unsweetened)
1 tablespoon honey

Blend ingredients until
smooth. Garnish with
orange slices. (Serves 2.)

PEACHY HONEY

2 peaches
2 teaspoons honey
½ cup pineapple
   chunks
1 cup crushed ice

Mix all ingredients until
smooth in blender. Garnish
with peach slices.
(Serves 2.)

ORANGE-MELON

1 cup diced
   cantaloupe
3 oranges
juice of ¼ lemon

Juice the cantaloupe,
squeeze the oranges and
combine the juices. Add
lemon juice. Mix well.
Serve over ice. Garnish
with orange slices.
(Serves 2.)

TANGERINE-APPLE

1 apple
1 tangerine

First juice the apple, then
squeeze the tangerine.

CANTALOUPE REFRESHER

¼ cup pineapple
   juice
1 cup cantaloupe
   chunks

Mix both ingredients in
blender until smooth.
Serve very cold. Garnish
with orange slices.
(Serves 2.)

DECEMBER LIFT

½ cup pineapple juice
  (*unsweetened*)
¼ cup raw cranberries
1 cup crushed ice
1 teaspoon honey

Combine ingredients in
blender and mix until
smooth. Garnish with
apple slices. (Serves 2.)

CRAN-APPLE

1 cup apple juice
¼ banana
¼ cup raw cran-
  berries

Whip ingredients in
blender until smooth.
Garnish with apple slices.
(Serves 2.)

GRAPE ZEST

1 apple
1 small bunch grapes,
  seedless or blue

Juice the apple, then the
grapes. Garnish with a
lemon peel.

FROSTY PINEAPPLE

1 cup pineapple juice
  (*unsweetened*)
1 teaspoon honey
½ apple
½ cup crushed ice

Mix the pineapple juice,
honey and apple in blender
until smooth. Add ice
slowly and blend until
drink is just mushy. Gar-
nish with orange slices.
(Serves 3.)

BANANA MILK

1 cup milk
1/8 teaspoon nutmeg
1 banana, sliced

Mix ingredients in blender until smooth. Add more milk if thinner drink is desired. (Serves 2.)

ORANGE-GRAPE

1/2 cup orange juice
juice of 1/2 lemon
1 tablespoon cream
2 tablespoons grape
   juice (unsweetened)
1 teaspoon honey

Mix ingredients together in blender until foamy. Garnish with orange slices.

FRUIT FLIP

small bunch grapes,
   any kind
1 wedge pineapple,
   2 inches wide,
   1 inch thick
5 strawberries

Juice all ingredients. Serve over crushed ice and garnish with fresh mint. (Serves 2.)

CURRIED TOMATO

3/4 cup tomato juice
pinch curry powder

Put both ingredients in blender and mix. Garnish with orange slice.

STRAWBERRY-MINT SHAKE

handful fresh mint
    leaves
2 cups water
1 cup strawberries
2 teaspoons honey

Put the mint and water in blender. Mix until smooth. Add other ingredients and whip until foamy. Garnish with whole sprigs of fresh mint. (Serves 4.)

FIG SHAKE

1 cup soybean milk,
    page 16
¼ cup fig juice

Whip ingredients until smooth in blender. (Serves 2.)

CHERRY SHAKE

½ pound Bing
    cherries, pitted
1 teaspoon honey
1 scoop vanilla ice
    cream
1 cup milk
¼ cup pecans

Mix ingredients in blender until foamy. (Serves 3.)

PEACH-FRUIT FLIP

¼ cup almond
  slivers
1 cup water
1 peach, pitted
1 apple
5 figs
1 cup crushed ice

Blend the almonds with
½ cup water until smooth.
Add remaining ½ cup
water and all ingredients
except ice. Mix until
smooth. Add ice and blend
until mushy. Garnish with
fresh mint. (Serves 4.)

FIG-SOYA SHAKE

1 cup soybean milk,
  page 16
3 figs

Put ingredients in blender
and mix until smooth and
foamy. Garnish with a
pinch of mace. (Serves 2.)

BANANA BUTTERSHAKE

1 cup buttermilk
3 drops vanilla or
  almond extract
1 banana, sliced

Put all ingredients in
blender and whip until
smooth. (Serves 2.)

ORANGE-GRAPEFRUIT FIZZ

1 cup orange juice
1 cup soda water
½ cup grapefruit
  juice

Mix ingredients in blender
until foamy. Serve over
crushed ice. Garnish with
fresh mint and orange
slices. (Serves 2.)

CRAN-ORANGE SHAKE

orange
½ cup raw cran-
 berries
½ cup vanilla ice
 cream

Squeeze the orange. Put
the juice with the other
ingredients in a blender.
Mix until smooth and
foamy. Garnish with lime
slices. (Serves 3.)

AVOCADO WHIP

small avocado,
 pitted and skinned
juice of ½ lemon
cup grapefruit
 juice

Mix ingredients in blender
until smooth. Add salt and
pepper or honey to taste.
Garnish with orange slices.
(Serves 2–3.)

PINEAPPLE-ORANGE FIZZ

tablespoon honey
tablespoons warm
 water
cup orange juice
¼ cup pineapple juice

1 egg white
¼ cup grapefruit juice
juice of ½ lemon
½ cup crushed ice

Mix honey and warm water together. Put all ingredients
in blender and mix until foamy. Garnish with slices of
fresh fruit. (Serves 3–4.)

PAPAYA-COCONUT SHAKE

1 ripe papaya
½ banana
2 tablespoons orange
    juice
juice of 1 lemon
3 tablespoons coco-
    nut milk from
    center of a fresh
    coconut

Cut the papaya and banana
into small pieces. Mix ingredients in blender until
smooth. Garnish with
orange slices. (Serves 2.)

PEACHY PARTY SHAKE

½ cup orange juice
½ cup milk
¼ teaspoon nutmeg
1 peach, pitted
½ cup vanilla ice
    cream

Whip ingredients in
blender until foamy. Gar-
nish with peach slices.
(Serves 2.)

APPLE JULEP

1 drop mint extract
2 apples
1 teaspoon lemon
    juice

Drop the mint extract int
the juicer. Juice the apple
and add the lemon juice
slowly. Garnish with a
sprig of fresh mint.

HONEY-FRUIT

1 grapefruit 1 orange ½ lemon 1 teaspoon honey	Squeeze the grapefruit, orange and lemon. Add the honey and mix well. Garnish with a sprig of fresh mint.

ORANGE BLOSSOM

1 cup strawberries 1 cup Bing cherries 2 oranges	Juice the strawberries and cherries. Squeeze the oranges. Combine the juices. Garnish with an orange slice.

APPLE BURST

1 apple 1 cup black grapes ½ cup pineapple juice (unsweetened)	Juice the apple and grapes. Add pineapple juice. Mix well. Garnish with an apple slice.

PINEAPPLE COCKTAIL

1 cup pineapple juice (unsweetened) pinch ground clove ¼ cup raw cran- berries	Blend all ingredients in blender until smooth. Garnish with sprigs of fresh mint. (Serves 2.)

APPLE-MELON COCKTAIL

½ cantaloupe
2 apples

Juice the fruits together.
Garnish with an apple
slice.

CRANBERRY COCKTAIL

½ cup cranberry
  juice
juice of 1 lemon
½ cup apple juice

Mix until foamy in
blender. Serve over ice
with orange slices as a
garnish. (Serves 2.)

CANTALOUPE NECTAR

¼ cup pineapple
  juice
1 cup cantaloupe
  chunks

Put the pineapple juice in
blender. Add cantaloupe,
a few chunks at a time.
Blend until smooth.
(Serves 2.)

EASY PINEAPPLE

½ cup pineapple
  juice
1 teaspoon honey
juice of 1 lemon

Combine ingredients and
garnish with an orange
slice.

FRUITY SHAKE

1 cup fresh mixed
   fruit (apples,
   peaches, pears,
   strawberries, blue-
   berries, etc.)
1 cup milk
6 ice cubes, crushed
1 tablespoon honey

Blend ingredients until
smooth. Garnish with
orange slices. (Serves 3.)

MINTED APRICOT NECTAR

1 cup apricot nectar
   (unsweetened)
sprig of fresh mint,
   chopped
pinch mace
1 teaspoon honey

Mix ingredients in blender
until smooth. Garnish with
a whole sprig of fresh
mint.

FRUIT-LIME WHIP

1 cup cantaloupe
   chunks
1½ tablespoons
   lime juice
1 cup strawberries

Mix ingredients in blender
until smooth. Garnish with
sprigs of fresh mint.
(Serves 2.)

FRUIT MILK

1 cup grapefruit juice
¼ cup milk
¼ cup orange juice

Mix ingredients in blender
until foamy. Garnish with
an orange slice.

PEACH FLIP

1 peach
1 cup pineapple juice
1 teaspoon honey

Cut the peach into pieces.
Whip all ingredients in
blender until foamy. Serve
over ice with peach slices
as a garnish. (Serves 2.)

SPICY CRAN-PINEAPPLE

½ cup pineapple juice
juice of 1 orange
pinch ground clove
¼ cup raw cranberries

½ teaspoon chopped
   fresh mint
pinch ground nutmeg

Mix ingredients in blender until smooth. Garnish with
orange slices. (Serves 2.)

HONEY-APPLE COCKTAIL

½ honeydew melon
½ cup apple juice

Combine the melon and
juice in blender and mix
until smooth. Serve over
crushed ice. Garnish with
orange slices. (Serves 2.)

ELDERBERRY DELIGHT

2 cups elderberries

Juice in extractor. Serve
over ice.

GRAPE COOLER

small bunch grapes
   (any kind)
5 strawberries
¼ cup pineapple juice

Juice the grapes and strawberries, combine with the pineapple juice and mix well.

BERRY FREEZE

1 pint blueberries
1 pint huckleberries

Juice together and serve over ice. Garnish with an orange slice. (Serves 2–3.)

STRAWAPPLE DRINK

11 strawberries
2 apples

First juice the strawberries, then the apples. Garnish with whole fresh strawberries.

FRUIT COCKTAIL

¼ honeydew
1 apple
½ cup strawberries
1 orange
1 grapefruit
⅓ cup pineapple juice
   (unsweetened)

Juice the honeydew, apple and strawberries. Squeeze the orange and grapefruit. Combine ingredients.
Serve over ice and garnish with fresh mint. (Serves 2–3.)

FRUIT FLIP

¼ *honeydew*
1 cup strawberries
½ *cup pineapple juice*
   (*unsweetened*)

Juice the honeydew and
strawberries. Add pine-
apple juice. Blend well.
(Serves 1–2.)

FRUIT-SHERBET SHAKE

½ *cup pineapple juice*
juice of ½ lemon
½ *cup orange juice*
½ *cup lemon sherbet*

Mix ingredients in blender
until smooth. Garnish with
sprigs of fresh mint.
(Serves 2.)

TANGERINE SPRITZ

4 tangerines
½ *pint strawberries*
juice of ¼ lemon

Squeeze the tangerines.
Juice the strawberries and
add lemon juice. Combine
juices and serve over
crushed ice. Garnish with
whole strawberries.

CITRUS SHAKE

½ *cup orange juice*
1 cup milk
1 cup grapefruit juice

Whip ingredients in
blender until foamy. Serve
over crushed ice. Garnish
with orange slices.
(Serves 3.)

PINEAPPLE WITH SEEDS

1 cup pineapple juice
1 tablespoon honey
¼ cup sunflower seeds

Mix ingredients in blender until smooth. Garnish with pineapple wedges. (Serves 2.)

VIRGIN MARY

1 cup tomato juice
½ teaspoon Worcestershire sauce
salt and pepper to taste
juice of ½ lemon
pinch ground mace, basil or oregano

Combine ingredients in blender and mix until smooth. Garnish with carrot sticks or cherry tomatoes. (Serves 1–2.)

APRICOT SHAKE

½ pound ripe apricots, pitted
1 cup milk

Soak apricots in milk until they are soft, adding enough water to cover fruit. Put ingredients in blender and whip until smooth. (Serves 3–4.)

PAPAYA MILK

1 papaya
coconut milk from center of 1 coconut

Juice the papaya and slowly add coconut milk through the juicer. (Serves 2.)

ORANGE BURST

1 cup strawberries
2 oranges

Juice the strawberries. Squeeze the oranges. Combine juices and serve over ice. Garnish with whole fresh strawberries.

STRAWBERRY SHAKE

1 pint strawberries
coconut milk from
  center of 1 coconut

Juice the strawberries and slowly add coconut milk through the juicer. Garnish with whole fresh strawberries.

SUNSHINE

1 papaya
juice of ½ lemon

Juice the papaya and add lemon juice. Mix well. Garnish with fresh mint.

STRAWBERRY TREAT

1 grapefruit
1 pint strawberries

Squeeze the grapefruit and juice the strawberries. Combine juices. Garnish with fresh mint.

FRUIT TEA

To a pot of hot tea with honey, add a finely diced fruit (apple, pear, peach, orange, grapes, etc.). Let the tea brew with the fruit in it. Drink hot or cold.

VEGETABLE &
FRUIT
COMBINATION
DRINKS

LEMON-CARROT

3 carrots
juice of ½ lemon

Juice carrots. Add lemon juice slowly through the extractor.

CARROT-COCONUT

2 carrots
¼ cup coconut milk from center of 1 coconut

Juice carrots. Slowly add coconut milk through extractor.

CABBAGE-PINEAPPLE

½ small cabbage
⅓ cup pineapple juice

Juice cabbage and add pineapple juice. Garnish with a pineapple wedge.

CARROT-POMEGRANATE

2 carrots
½ pomegranate

Juice both ingredients. Garnish with an orange slice.

TOMATO COOLER

2 tomatoes
1 slice lemon
1 handful beet tops

Juice all ingredients.
(Serves 2.)

VEGETABLE COCKTAIL

½ small tomato
1 stalk celery
½ green pepper
2 carrots

Juice all ingredients,
carrots last. Garnish
with a sprig of parsley.
(Serves 1–2.)

CARROT-ORANGE

2 carrots
1 orange

Juice carrots and squeeze
the orange. Combine
juices. Garnish with an
orange slice.

CARROT-CELERY

1½ carrots
2 stalks celery
a few drops of lemon
    juice

Juice both vegetables and
add the lemon juice. Gar-
nish with a lemon slice.

BEET BURST

leaves from one head
    of cauliflower
½ beet
⅔ cup pineapple
    juice

Juice the cauliflower leaves
first, followed by the beet.
Combine with pineapple
juice. Garnish with a pineapple wedge.

VEGETABLE-ORANGE STINGER

4 leaves romaine
  lettuce
1 small beet
2 carrots
½ orange

Juice the lettuce, beet and carrots. Squeeze the orange. Combine ingredients. Garnish with an orange slice.

COMBINATION COOLER

½ apple
2 carrots
½ orange

Juice the apple, then the carrots. Squeeze the orange. Combine ingredients. Garnish with an orange slice.

LEMONY BEET

2 beets
lemon juice

Juice the beets and add lemon juice to taste.

SPINACH-PINEAPPLE JULEP

sprig fresh pepper-
  mint or spearmint*
1 handful spinach
1 cup pineapple juice

First juice the mint, then the spinach. Slowly add the pineapple juice through the extractor. Serve over ice and garnish with whole sprigs of mint. (Serves 2.)

* Fresh peppermint and spearmint are very hard to find, but should be used whenever possible.

CUCUMBER-ORANGE

3 oranges
1 small cucumber

Juice oranges and cucumber together. Garnish with orange slices. (Serves 2–3.)

RED CABBAGE FLOAT

1 handful red cabbage
½ cup pineapple juice

Juice the cabbage and slowly add the pineapple juice.

COCONUT COOLER

1 beet
2 carrots
3 tablespoons coconut
   juice from a fresh
   coconut

Juice the beet and carrots and add coconut juice slowly. Garnish with a piece of fresh coconut.

APPLE-CELERY

1 apple
3 stalks celery

Juice the apple first, then the celery. Garnish with a slice of apple.

CARROT-BEET DELIGHT

½ apple
½ small beet
2 carrots

Juice the apple first, then the beet and carrots. Garnish with an apple slice.

DANDELION HEAVEN

1 small handful dandelion leaves 2 carrots 2 oranges juice of ½ lemon	Juice the dandelion leaves first, then the other ingredients. Garnish with orange slices. (Serves 2–3.)

ORANGE-BEET

1 medium beet 2 oranges	Juice the beet, squeeze the oranges and combine the juices well. Garnish with an orange slice.

VEGETABLE-FRUIT

2-inch wedge of pineapple 3 carrots ½ orange	Juice the pineapple, then the carrots. Squeeze the orange. Mix together. Garnish with an orange slice.

PINEAPPLE FLOAT

2 small beets ⅔ cup pineapple juice	Juice the beets, then add pineapple juice. Mix well.

CELERY SUNSHINE

1 apple 2 stalks celery 1 carrot	Juice the apple first, then the celery and carrot. Garnish with an apple slice.

RAINBOW CARROT

5 leaves romaine
  lettuce
½ pomegranate
2 carrots

Juice the lettuce first,
then the pomegranate
and carrots.

FRUIT SURPRISE

½ orange
1 apple
½ beet
1 carrot

Squeeze the orange first,
then juice all other
ingredients. Garnish with
orange slices. (Serves 2.)

PINEAPPLE FIZZ

1 carrot
2 stalks celery
⅓ cup pineapple juice

Juice the carrot and celery
and add the pineapple
juice. Garnish with an
orange slice.

TROPICAL COOLER

½ cup grape juice
¼ cup pineapple juice
1 carrot, finely diced
1 teaspoon honey

½ cup apple juice
¼ cup chopped orange
juice of ½ lemon

Whip ingredients in blender until smooth. Garnish with
orange slices. (Serves 3.)

TOMATO FANCY

1 cup tomato juice
1 carrot, diced
½ teaspoon chopped
  parsley

1 celery stalk, chopped
3 sprigs watercress,
  chopped
½ teaspoon lemon juice

Whip all ingredients in blender until smooth. Add salt
and pepper to taste. (Serves 2.)

CARROT-ORANGE WHIP

½ cup orange juice
½ cup milk
dash cinnamon
1 carrot, diced
1 teaspoon honey

Mix ingredients in
blender until smooth.
Garnish with cinnamon
sticks. (Serves 2.)

ORANGE-SPINACH TREAT

1 orange
5 sprigs parsley
1 handful spinach

Juice ingredients in the
order given. Garnish with
an orange slice.

PAPAYA COCKTAIL

1 small papaya
¼ green pepper, finely
  chopped
a few drops of Worcester-
  shire sauce

½ cup tomato juice
2 teaspoons lemon
  juice

Put all ingredients in blender and mix until smooth. Garnish with cucumber slices. (Serves 2.)

TANGY TOMATO

½ cup tomato juice
3 drops onion juice*
1 teaspoon soy sauce
½ cup cucumber
  juice
juice of ¼ lemon

Mix ingredients in blender
until smooth. Garnish
with cucumber slices.
(Serves 2.)

* Make onion juice by squeezing onion through a garlic press.

CURRIED SPINACH DELIGHT

½ pound spinach
1 small tomato
pinch curry powder

First juice the spinach,
then the tomato. Mix
curry powder in the
finished drink.

TOMATO-CELERY

1 handful spinach
3 stalks celery
1 small tomato
juice of ½ lemon

Juice the spinach first. Add
the lemon juice slowly.
Garnish with a lemon slice.

BEET FLIP

2 medium beets
1 small apple

Juice both ingredients together. Garnish with an
orange slice.

CUCUMBER COOLER

½ cucumber
2 stalks celery
3 radishes
¼ cup pineapple juice
(unsweetened)

Juice the vegetables and add the pineapple juice.

APPLE-BEET

1 medium beet
2 small apples

Juice both ingredients together. Garnish with an apple slice.

SPINACH-PINEAPPLE

3 handfuls spinach
½ cup pineapple juice
(unsweetened)
a few drops lemon
juice

Juice the spinach. Add the pineapple juice and the lemon juice. Mix well. Garnish with a slice of lemon.

PEPPER TINGLE

6 blue grapes
2 stalks celery
¼ green pepper
1 carrot
½ small beet

First juice the grapes, then the celery, pepper, carrot and beet. Mix well. Garnish with an orange slice.

GRAPE-BEET

1 cup seedless grapes
1 medium beet

First juice the grapes, then the beet.

SPINACH-ORANGE

8 sprigs watercress
½ pound spinach
1 orange

First juice the watercress, then the spinach. Squeeze the orange. Combine all juices. Garnish with an orange slice.

APPLE-SPINACH

2 handfuls spinach
1 apple

Juice the spinach first. Garnish with an apple slice.

HONEY-RADISH

4 radishes
¾ cup pineapple juice (unsweetened)
honey

Juice the radishes and add the pineapple juice. Mix in honey to taste.

CELERY COOLER

3 stalks celery
1 grapefruit

Juice the celery, squeeze the grapefruit and combine.

VEGETABLE REFRESHER

1½ cups tomato juice
juice of ¼ lemon
rind of ¼ lemon, cut up
¼ small onion, chopped
1 sprig parsley, chopped

¼ green pepper, chopped
1 stalk celery with small amount of leaves, chopped

Put ingredients in blender and mix until smooth. Garnish with chopped parsley. (Serves 3–4.)

PINEAPPLE-BASIL

1 cup pineapple juice
  (*unsweetened*)
juice of ½ lemon
¼ cup finely chopped
  carrot
¼ teaspoon basil

Combine ingredients in
blender and mix until
smooth. Garnish with
lime slices. (Serves 2.)

ORANGE ROYALE

¾ cup orange juice
2 tablespoons papaya
  syrup concentrate*
½ teaspoon cinnamon
½ cup sliced carrots

Mix ingredients in blender
until smooth. Garnish with
orange slices. (Serves 2–3.)

* Papaya syrup concentrate can be purchased in a health food store.

MAKE YOUR OWN COMBINATION

In preparing your own concoctions, keep in mind the following: Fruit juices can be taken alone or combined with any other fruit juice; when combining with a vegetable juice, only one kind of fruit juice should be used, and whatever vegetable combination you wish. Apple juice is the best fruit to add to vegetables and a good base for most combination drinks.

A combination of raw fruit juice and a solid raw fruit is an aid to digestion and stomach-cleansing. Taken early in the day, such a combination works like a broom, sweeping through the digestive tract and opening the way for the body to receive the day's food.

✿ YOGURT & MILK DRINKS

ALMOND YOGURT

1 cup plain yogurt
1 teaspoon honey
1 cup milk
2 teaspoons almond slivers

Put all ingredients in blender and mix until smooth. Garnish with a pinch of nutmeg. (Serves 2.)

YOGURT WITH ROSEWATER

1 cup ice water
⅛ cup raw sugar or honey
a few drops of rosewater*
¼ cup plain yogurt
pinch nutmeg

Whip ingredients together in blender until smooth. Garnish with a small tea rose in season. (Serves 1–2.)

* Rosewater can be purchased at a health food store or a drug store.

YOGURT PLUS

½ cup fresh fruit
1½ teaspoons wheat
   germ
1 cup liquid yogurt*
1 tablespoon nutri-
   tional yeast or
   protein powder
1½ teaspoons soy
   flour

Mix ingredients in blender
until smooth. Garnish with
fresh fruit. (Serves 2.)

* Yogurt can be bought in a liquid state in a health food store, or
mix plain yogurt with equal parts of milk.

PINEAPPLE-APRICOT YOGURT

½ cup pineapple juice
   (unsweetened)
2 tablespoons maple
   syrup

¼ cup apricot nectar
   (unsweetened)
½ cup liquid yogurt

Mix ingredients in blender until smooth. Garnish with
orange slices. (Serves 2.)

ORANGE YOGURT

½ cup orange juice
½ teaspoon powdered
   fruit rind
½ cup plain yogurt
pinch ground mace

Whip ingredients together
in blender until smooth.
Garnish with an orange
slice.

TOMATO YOGURT

½ cup plain yogurt   Blend ingredients until
1 dulse leaf,* chopped   smooth. (Serves 2.)
½ cup tomato juice
½ teaspoon soy sauce

* Dulse is an edible weed, known in Ireland and Scotland, and now
most commonly used in Hawaii.

GRAPE YOGURT

½ cup yogurt   Mix ingredients in blender
½ cup grape juice   until smooth. Garnish with
   (unsweetened)   orange slices. (Serves 2.)

BLUEBERRY YOGURT

½ cup plain yogurt   Mix ingredients in blender
½ cup milk   until smooth. Garnish with
½ cup fresh blue-   sprigs of fresh mint.
   berries   (Serves 2.)
2 teaspoons honey

PAPAYA YOGURT

1 ripe papaya   Cut papaya into small
¾ cup yogurt   pieces and blend with
1 tablespoon orange   other ingredients until
   juice   smooth. Garnish with
¼ cup honey   nutmeg. (Serves 3.)

APPLE-PRUNE

½ cup prune juice
1 teaspoon plain
  yogurt
½ cup apple juice
1 teaspoon almond
  slivers

Whip all ingredients in
blender until smooth.
Garnish with apple slices.
(Serves 2.)

PINEAPPLE-COCONUT

½ cup coconut milk,
  page 16
½ cup pineapple juice
  (unsweetened)
1 tablespoon yogurt

Mix ingredients in blender
until smooth. Garnish with
orange slices. (Serves 2.)

MINT YOGURT

½ cup plain yogurt
peel of 1 lemon, chopped
  fine
1 teaspoon finely chopped
  fresh mint

1 cup water
pinch chili powder
salt and pepper to
  taste

Whip ingredients in blender until smooth. Garnish with
sprigs of fresh mint. (Serves 2.)

HIGH-PROTEIN DRINK

5 ounces ice water
1 tablespoon powdered
  milk
1½ teaspoons protein
  powder
1 tablespoon unsalted
  nuts

1½ teaspoons sunflower
  seeds
dash cinnamon
½ teaspoon honey

Put water, milk and protein powder into blender and mix

until smooth. Add nuts, seeds and cinnamon and blend at low speed until smooth. Add honey and blend all ingredients until foamy. Garnish with an orange slice.

CAROB-HONEY DRINK

1 cup milk
1½ tablespoons carob
  powder
¼ teaspoon honey
⅛ teaspoon vanilla
  extract

Put all ingredients in blender and mix until smooth. (Serves 2.)

HONEY EGGNOG

1 cup milk
1½ teaspoons honey
1 egg
⅓ cup powdered
  milk

Put ingredients in blender and whip until smooth. Garnish with a sprinkle of nutmeg. (Serves 2.)

ANISE MILK SHAKE

1 cup milk
1½ teaspoons honey
¼ teaspoon anise
  seed
6 tablespoons
  powdered milk

Put ingredients in blender and mix until smooth. (Serves 2.)

GINGER-MILK DRINK

1 cup soybean milk,
    page 16
¼ teaspoon ground
    ginger
1½ teaspoons honey
¼ teaspoon ground
    nutmeg

Blend all ingredients
until smooth. Serve with
sugared ginger as a
garnish. (Serves 2.)

HONEY-MILK DRINK

1 cup hot milk
2 teaspoons honey

Blend until smooth. Gar-
nish with a sprinkle of
nutmeg.

MALTED MILK DRINK

1 cup hot milk
2 teaspoons malt
    extract

Blend ingredients until
smooth in blender. Serve
hot or cold.

ALMOND-COFFEE DRINK

1 cup strong coffee
½ cup soda water
¼ cup milk
2 drops almond
    extract

Put ingredients in blender
and mix until foamy.
Garnish with a dash of
cinnamon. (Serves 2.)

COFFEE

🌺 ORIGINS

*O, coffee, thou dispellest the cares of the great and
bringest back those who wander from the paths of
knowledge! Coffee is our gold, and in the place of
its illusions we are in the enjoyment of the best
and noblest society. Every care vanishes when the
cup-bearer presents the delicious chalice to our lips.
It circulates freely through our veins and will not
rankle there. Grief cannot exist where it grows and
sorrow humbles itself before its powers.*
—Ancient Arabic ceremonial invocation

The early history of coffee is somewhat obscure, but legend has added a wealth of detail to the sketchy historical facts.

The virtues of the coffee plant were recognized first in Ethiopia around 800 A.D. by the semi-savage tribes who wandered across the desert. To free themselves for surprise attacks, these nomads traveled light. The only food they carried was coffee. The beans were roasted and mashed, mixed with grease, rolled into small balls and stored in leather bags. One coffee ball was sufficient nourishment for an entire day and was considered better than either bread or meat because the tribes had to operate under battle conditions and the coffee got them "up" or "high" for the fight as well as serving as nourishment.

From its very discovery, coffee was most appreciated for its druglike effect. Both its adherents and detractors regarded it as a drug.

The Ethiopians introduced coffee to Arabia about 1200 A.D., and from there many stories emanate about the amazing "highs" induced by the plant. One such tale is of the monks who heard from their shepherd of the weird and exciting reaction the local goats displayed whenever they browsed at a certain kind of tree. The monks then prepared a brew from the beans on the tree, which had the effect of allowing them to stay up all night for their prayers. The drug was soon officially sanctioned by the Mufti of Aden and adopted by an elite group of professional people, artisans and night-travelers.

The Arabs believed that the brew purified the blood, alleviated stomach aches and aroused the spirits. Coffee soon became a favorite drink not just of those who needed to stay awake at night. Conflicts arose with the orthodox Mohammedan priesthood, who held coffee to be an intoxicating beverage and threatened divine retribution to all "coffee addicts." Nevertheless, coffee drinking increased.

As coffee spread throughout Arabia, public coffee-houses were established and became centers for activities that had not existed before their advent: political organizations, business relationships, poetry readings, organized gossip. Newspapers were as yet hundreds of years in the future, and the introduction of coffee in effect created a new kind of communications construct centered around the social consumption of the brew.

Prohibition continually followed the spread of coffee drinking. Around the year 1500, the governing authorities in Arabia attempted to eliminate coffee drinking on the old grounds that it was an intoxicant. But this was a political maneuver, putting the onus of the prohibition on the religious sector, when in reality the government itself was worried about the new social and cultural configurations that by their very nature were the enemy of the established institutions. In 1510 the governor of Cairo imposed a ban on coffee drinking which was in effect for about thirty years until it was rescinded as a result of popular demand. The brew was brought to Damascus in 1530, and to Constantinople in 1554, where it became so popular that refusal to supply a wife with a daily ration of coffee was considered valid grounds for divorce.

Coffee reached Marseilles in 1660, and the first coffee shop was opened there in 1671. Around that time the French royal family adopted the beverage, importing vast quantities at enormous cost and making it the fashionable drink of the age.

The use of coffee in England predates its introduction in France. The earliest account says that it was offered for sale in 1640 by a man called Jacob the Jew who lived in Oxford. An early advertisement for "cophee" in 1663 stated: "It quickens the spirits, and makes the heart lightsome, suppresseth the fumes exceedingly, and, therefore, is good against headache, prevents cough and consumption, and is excellent for the cure of gout, dropsy, scurvey, hypochondria, and the like."

As was the case in Arabia, the English and French coffeehouses became news centers where intelligent men of the time gathered to discuss political, business, social and artistic opinions and facts. Once again, several brief but abortive attempts were made to close down the coffee shops, but the public prevailed.

The establishment of coffeehouses was part of the early history of the United States, where the beverage is today used more extensively than anywhere else in the world.

DEVELOPMENT OF THE COFFEE DRINK

The coffee we drink today has its roots in the ancient methods that semi-civilized men devised to extract flavors from the beans of the coffee shrub. The Arabs were the first to prepare it in liquid form. They made a drink called *kishre* by pounding the beans with stones, placing them in boiling water, adding ground cardamoms, cinnamon and ginger, and then simmering the mixture for half an hour over a low fire.

The Turks regarded coffee as their national beverage. They ground the beans as fine as flour and placed them in a pot of cold water which they brought almost to the boiling point and then served without any additions.

The Egyptians used the Turkish grind, added an equal quantity of sugar and brought the mixture to a full boil, not once but several times, allowing for cooling in between in order to create a thick consistency.

In Java, coffee is still made from the leaves, which contain a larger amount of caffeine than the beans. The leaves are roasted and cured and then prepared in the same manner as tea.

The Europeans added spices and, occasionally, liquors. In certain royal households, coffee was even brewed with champagne. Cream and sugar are rather recent innovations. When Europeans first encountered coffee, spices were the established flavorings. Sugar and molasses were added to suit tastes unaccustomed to such bitterness. Milk was added around 1660 by the Dutch ambassador to China, who imitated Chinese tea by adding milk and opened the way for café au lait, and the coffee "regular" that is consumed in such vast quantities today.

The physiological action is directed chiefly to the nervous system, producing a warm cordial feeling in the stomach, which is quickly followed by a well-diffused and agreeable nervous excitement extending itself to the cerebral functions, giving rise to increased vigor to the imagination and intellect without causing any subsequent stupor or confusion of ideas, such as are so characteristic of other narcotics. It produces contentment of mind, allays hunger, mental and bodily weariness, increases the capacity for work, makes man forget his troubles and anxieties, enabling those who use it judiciously to endure unusual fatigue and remain a long time without food or sleep, as well as to preserve their temper and cheerfulness.

The above quotation might sound like an apologia for pot smoking but is actually a turn-of-the-century medical report on the benefits of coffee drinking. It's interesting to note that while today coffee is universally accepted as a regular part of our diet, in the past it was considered medicinal and regarded more highly for its stimulant effect than for its value as a drink.

Caffeine, which is the stimulating agent in the coffee bean, differs from drugs and alcohol in that it is a pure stimulant with no second stage of depression and does not produce a need for continual increase of dosage. Most important, it has no cumulative action and is rapidly eliminated. Taken in moderation, it is simply not harmful.

Caffeine was responsible for a long list of medicinal uses of coffee as late as the turn of this century. It was said to be an anti-soporific, a stimulant for persons res

ued from starvation or intense cold, a digestive aid, a
ure for chronic rheumatism (when taken with black pep-
er) and, most interestingly, a room deodorant and dis-
infectant; fresh-roasted coffee passed through a room on
dish instantly absorbs noxious odors.

TABLE OF COMPARATIVE VALUES FOR CAFFEINE PER
5-OUNCE SERVING

	CAFFEINE
Coffee	90–125 mg
Decaffeinated Coffee	3.3 mg
Tea	30–70 mg
Breakfast Cocoa	1.1–3.2 mg
Chocolate	7.8 mg
Cola	37 mg

Coffee is grown on a tree or shrub which produces a
ruit known as the "berry." Inside the berry are two beans,
ach surrounded by silvery skin, which in turn is enclosed
a a cherrylike pulpy substance.

It takes about five years for the coffee tree to produce
s first full crop, at which time white blossoms appear.
he berries which appear after the flowers have fallen off
re picked by hand and transported to nearby processing
lants.

At the plant, the beans are separated from the berries
y one of two methods: wet or dry. In either case, the
rst step is to wash the berries and separate them from
vigs, leaves, etc.

The dry method is used mainly in Brazil and in coun-
ies where water is scarce. The berries are spread out
a dry ground for a few weeks, raked daily to ensure even
rying and then heaped and covered at night for protec-
on against moisture. When dry, they are processed
rough a milling machine to remove both the dried husk
nd the inner silver skin.

The wet method is used in countries where the water

supply is plentiful. The berries are put into machines which remove the outside pulp and expose a sticky material surrounding the beans; then transferred to concrete tanks to remove this material; then poured into washing machines which cleanse them with constantly changing clear water; then drained and dried; and finally processed through a hulling machine to extricate the beans.

At this stage the beans are graded for size, type and quality and packed in 132-pound bags for export. The finished coffee that reaches its destination is "green coffee," which consists of beans that are green or blue-green and can be stored for a long period.

The different grades of coffee fall into two general categories: *arabica,* which is not grown in Arabia but comes from Central and South America and has a rich, mellow flavor; and *robusta,* a less flavorsome, less expensive variety which comes from the lowlands of Africa. About 58 percent of the world's green coffee is from Central and South America (Brazil 22 percent, Colombia 14 percent), and 37 percent comes from the African continent. More than half of the total is imported by the United States. The green beans arrive in this country and are blended, roasted and packed for shipment to wholesale and retail outlets.

There are over one hundred different coffee growths from twenty-odd countries throughout the world. The bag of coffee that is purchased in the specialty store or supermarket is not the product of one or even two of these growths, but will contain a blend of at least eight to ten varieties.

Flavor, aroma and price are the considerations going into a particular coffee blend. Coffee tasters sample from a vast combination of the different varieties and grades within these varieties. The taster considers the acidity (in coffee terms, the brightness of the flavor accent), body, color, aroma and flavor. A typical blend might include the following: 40 percent high-grade Santos from Brazil

40 percent Medellins from Colombia and 20 percent Maracaibos from Venezuela. While the blends for whole roasted beans are rather simple, the commercially ground coffees, which are sold by major packagers in vacuum cans, are much more complicated, sometimes combining forty to fifty different coffees.

When the beans arrive in this country, they go through a process of controlled heating called "roasting," which develops the distinctive coffee aroma and taste. During this process the beans expand to about twice their original size and turn from green to brown. The longer the beans are roasted, the deeper their color. The darker roast has absolutely no effect on the strength or stimulation of the brew but merely creates a darker-colored beverage.

BUYING COFFEE

There's no comparison to picking out your own blen of whole roasted beans, grinding them at home, and pre paring them while the freshness and aroma are still intac Bear in mind that the commercially ground pre-package coffee brands are processed that way for the convenienc of the seller, not the purchaser. By all means try to g the real thing and do it yourself. Any well-stocked sp cialty food store will carry at least a few coffee blends i the whole roasted bean. The following blends are thos most generally available:

African Arabica: highly flavorful and aromatic
African Robusta: mildest and lightest of all
Brazilian Santos: robust, somewhat "sweet" and heav bodied
Central American: flavorful, grand bouquet
Colombian Medellin: full-bodied, rich, "winy"
Ethiopian Djimmah: full-bodied, aromatic
French Roast (dark): the darkest and most bitter ble —used in espresso blends and to build strength as mix for regular coffees. For demitasse
French Roast (light): slightly overroasted blend with o surface (for demitasse) which brings out nutlike flav when mixed with regular coffees
Italian Roast: medium-strong

Jamaican Blue Mountain: rich, mellow blend

Java: mild, but rich

Kenya: medium-strength African

Kona: mild Hawaiian

Mexican: slightly smoky flavor

Mocha: unique, sharp flavor, from Aden

Mocha Java: heavier than mocha, more aromatic and smoother

Peaberry: medium-strength African

Spanish Roast: a demitasse blend lighter than the French roasts

Tanganyikan: medium-to-mild African

Turkish Blend: full-bodied, extremely strong

Each of the above blends has its own distinctive flavor. The differences among them can be considerable. The best approach is to sample them until you find the blend that best suits you.

Many areas of the country do not have their own coffee stores or specialty shops which carry whole-bean roasted coffee. In such areas, the whole-bean coffee is sometimes available in the food departments of large department stores. Also some of the large chain supermarkets carry this product.

 # GRIND

Coffee cannot be brewed from the whole roasted bean and still provide a delicious taste. The particular grind adapts the bean for one of a number of preparation processes so that the maximum flavor will be extracted through contact with hot water. If the grind is too coarse, the water passes through too quickly. If it is too fine or powdery, the coffee will taste bitter. The grind relates directly to the amount of time the coffee should be in contact with the hot water:

fine grind (vacuum)	1–4 minutes
medium grind (drip)	4–6 minutes
coarse or "regular" (percolator)	6–8 minutes

Coffee can be ground at home in any variety of hand or electric grinder. Some of the more expensive models have exact-timing devices to ensure that the grind will be as desired.

☙ MAKING COFFEE

The ideal cup of coffee is a myth. It is strictly a matter of personal taste. But there are a number of important steps to follow in order to get the best brew out of the coffee beans.

1. STORING COFFEE Fresh-roasted beans are usually sold in bags. They should be transferred to a container with a sealable lid and kept in the refrigerator until they are to be used. Allow them to stand at room temperature for about a half-hour before grinding or brewing; otherwise the temperature of the coffee will be too low. If more than one bag of beans is purchased at a time, the extra beans should be transferred to storage containers and kept in the freezer where they will stay fresh for months. Never prepare a brew from beans just removed from the freezer. Always use beans which are at room temperature. The best bet is to have one "ready" jar in the refrigerator. Remember to keep the container securely sealed, as coffee, which was once widely used as a room deodorant, quickly assimilates odors from other foods.

2. WATER The composition of water (hard or soft) has an effect on coffee. Hard water flows through the coffee grounds faster than soft water. Thus, slightly more coffee is needed for hard water than soft water. Cold water should always be used because hot-water pipes accumulate mineral deposits that can affect the taste of the brew. In all methods of preparation, the water temperature should be near 200° or just under the boiling point as the water comes in contact with the coffee grounds. At higher temperatures, the chemical components tend to break down, and at lower temperatures the beverage is too cool for best drinking. Take into account the temperature of cold cups as well as the addition of milk or cream and sugar as elements that will lower the temperature of the coffee.

3. MEASURING   The coffee/water ratio is always the same, regardless of type of coffee maker and method of preparation. For every cup of coffee, *1 standard coffee measure (2 level tablespoons) to 6 ounces of water*. This is standard in all cases save one, the preparation of demitasse, which uses 3 level tablespoons to each 6 ounces of water.

4. TIMING   Percolator method: 6 to 8 minutes; drip method: 4 to 6 minutes; vacuum method: 1 to 4 minutes. Too little time and the coffee will be weak, too long and it will be bitter. Always make coffee full-strength and use the coffee maker to as near to capacity as possible.

5. SERVING   Coffee is brewed, not boiled. Boiling coffee ruins its flavor. Always serve coffee immediately after brewing. Coffee can be held for up to one hour (but not much longer) at 185–190°. Never reheat coffee which has been allowed to cool. This breaks down the chemical components and results in an undesirable flavor.

METHODS OF PREPARATION

THE DRIP METHOD This method (and the vacuum method) are superior to percolation, as the water passes through the ground coffee with the greatest efficiency. In the drip method, boiling water is poured into an upper container and trickles slowly through coffee grounds, extracting the coffee brew as it drips into a lower bowl. There are three types of drip makers.

Regular Drip Coffee Maker

1. Preheat pot by rinsing with boiling water.
2. Measure drip-grind coffee into coffee basket and replace upper section.
3. Bring water to a boil, and let it cool for about four minutes. The water should not be more than 200° when it makes contact with the coffee. Boiling water extracts bitter elements from the coffee. A slightly lower temperature improves the brew. Pour the correct amount of water into upper section. Cover. When dripping is complete, remove upper section and stir coffee.

Filter-Cone Type Drip Pot

This is a very desirable method of coffee preparation, using specially treated filter paper to extract sediments and oils that can negatively affect the brew.

1. Preheat pot by rinsing in hot water.
2. Place proper filter in upper cone and add *regular grind* coffee (this method requires a coarser grind than the regular drip coffee maker).
3. The first portion of water that hits the coffee should be a small amount which wets through the coffee but does not float it. Filter manufacturers claim that "this portion of water is to disturb the air and to blast the cells of the woody structure of the coffee."

4. Allow to stand for one minute. Continue by slowly adding water in small amounts, never allowing the liquid level in the filter cone to rise much above that of the dry coffee. This ensures that all the water is in contact with all the coffee, and that the brew is emitted through the very tip of the cone. When adding the water, use a circular motion.
5. Remove filter cone and serve.

Electric Filter-Cone Type Drip Pot

This is a relatively new item on the market and a nearly foolproof as well as convenient method of coffee preparation. The principle is the same as in the preceding manual filter method, except that the water is poured into a separate compartment, heated electrically, and forced up through a spout in even amounts to trickle through the coffee grounds, which are held in either a chemically treated paper filter cone or a nylon filter. The brew seeps through into a waiting pot which stands on a hot plate maintaining the coffee at a temperature of 185° to 190°. Some models have a high-speed heating element which allows for the complete brewing of eight cups of coffee in as little as two to three minutes.

THE VACUUM METHOD Steam from boiling water in a lower bowl creates pressure which forces water into an upper bowl, where it gently bubbles through the coffee grounds. As the lower bowl cools, a vacuum is created that pulls the brew through a filter into the lower bowl.

1. Remove upper bowl and insert filter. Add fine-grind coffee.
2. Bring cold water to boil in lower bowl. Remove from heat.
3. Insert upper bowl, twisting slightly for tight fit. Return to reduced heat.
4. Let water rise into upper bowl and mix with coffee for

one minute, stirring with a zigzag motion for twenty seconds.

5. Remove from heat. When brew returns to lower bowl (2 minutes), remove upper bowl and serve.

THE PERCOLATOR METHOD   This is a poor method for brewing coffee. Household coffee percolation spoils the coffee aroma by steam distillation and leaves strong-tasting soluble residues. In this method, the water bubbles up through a tube and sprays over the coffee in a basket at the top of the tube. As it trickles through the grounds, the coffee is extracted. However, the brew has actually been boiled, and this spoils its taste. Boiling brings out the tannic acid in the coffee bean and makes the brew bitter as well as cloudy.

Be careful to check out the water-level markings on a percolator; they are often inaccurate.

Range-Top Percolator

1. Remove coffee basket and stem. Fill basket with regular-grind coffee.
2. Bring measured water to a boil in percolator. Remove from heat.
3. Insert coffee basket. Cover. Return to low heat. Water level should always be below bottom of basket.
4. Percolate for 6 to 8 minutes. Remove coffee basket and stem before serving.

Automatic Percolator

Follow manufacturer's instructions. In many such models the brewing time takes up to 20 minutes, resulting in overbrewed coffee. End manually, if necessary, after 8 minutes.

ESPRESSO MACHINES & MACCHINETTAS   Italian espresso uses steam pressure to brew the rich nut-flavored coffee. Small electric models are available for

home use. The Italian version of the drip coffee maker
is the *macchinetta*. Use it like any drip maker.

HOBO (OR "COWBOY") COFFEE   Using only a pot
or pan and some water.

1. Warm an ordinary pot or pan in hot water.
2. Measure into pot 4 tablespoons of coffee for each pint
   of boiling water.
3. Pour on water, place lid on pot and keep hot.
4. After 4 minutes lift lid and touch coffee, which is floating on top, with a spoon. After a moment it will settle
   to the bottom. Serve.

INSTANT COFFEE   Instant coffees are water-soluble.
They are not really special grinds but are composed of
tiny crystals of very strongly brewed fresh coffee that has
been dehydrated. When boiling water is added, the crystals
turn into a beverage once again.

"Freeze-dried" differs from regular instant in that the
brewed coffee is frozen and then dried by vaporization
in an effort to preserve more of the freshness, flavor and
aroma of the original brew.

CLEANLINESS

It is absolutely essential to maintain a clean coffee maker.
Coffee contains oil which forms an almost invisible film
on the inner walls of the pot. Unless completely removed
it will turn bad and spoil the taste of the subsequent cup
of coffee. After making a pot of coffee, wash all the parts
of the pot in hot water with a mild detergent. Rinse with
clear water. Scald with very hot water before using again.
From time to time it is advisable to take the coffee maker
apart and scrub all the parts.

COFFEE BEVERAGES

In addition to the "simple" cup of coffee, there are a multiplicity of refinements that have evolved through man's use of the coffee bean. These coffee and coffee-flavored beverages include iced coffee, carbonated drinks, liqueurs and foreign preparations calling for whipped cream, lemon peel, cinnamon, cloves, chocolate, milk, etc. The following recipes provide a sampling.

TURKISH COFFEE

⅓ cup water
2 teaspoons sugar

1 teaspoon pulverized
(very finely ground)
dark-roast coffee

Heat all ingredients in an *ibrik,* the long-handled Turkish coffee pot. Allow coffee to rise until it froths to the top. Remove from heat for a moment until coffee settles down. Then repeat the process two more times. Allow coffee to settle, and serve immediately. Never let coffee boil. Connoisseurs prepare Turkish coffee at the table over an alcohol lamp and add no sweeteners to the final brew. None of the ordinary degrees of grind are fine enough for this brew. The beans must be *completely pulverized* by the grinder. (Serves 1.)

ARMENIAN COFFEE

2 cups cold water
2 tablespoons pul-
  verized dark-roast
  coffee
1 tablespoon powdered
  sugar

Prepare the same way as
Turkish coffee. (Serves 2.)

CAFÉ AU LAIT/CAFÉ CON LECHE

1 cup strong coffee
1 cup hot milk

Holding pot of coffee in
one hand and pot of hot
milk in the other, pour
them out simultaneously
into 2 cups. (Serves 2.)

INDIA COFFEE

2 tablespoons fine-
  grind mocha coffee
4 cups boiling water
1 tablespoon rosewater

Add coffee to boiling
water, bring to a full boil
and stir in rosewater.
Pour into small cups.
(Serves 3-4.)

HOT MOCHA JAVA

1 cup hot coffee
1 cup hot cocoa
whipped cream or
  marshmallows

Heat coffee and cocoa
together, but do not boil.
Pour into cups and top
with whipped cream or
marshmallows. (Serves 2.)

CAFÉ CACAO

1 cup hot coffee	Combine coffee with
1 jigger crème de	crème de cacao. Top
cacao	with whipped cream.
whipped cream	(Serves 1.)

CAFFÈ CAPPUCCINO

1 cup hot milk	Add steaming-hot milk
1 cup Italian demi-	to Italian demitasse coffee,
tasse coffee	half and half. Serve with
cinnamon	cinnamon on top.
	(Serves 2.)

CAFFE ESPRESSO

Espresso is made with a very fine grind dark-roast coffee and prepared in a special machine which provides fast filtration. Serve in demitasse cups with or without sugar and a twist of lemon peel.

CAFÉ ROYALE

Place a lump of sugar in a demitasse cup. Fill halfway with strong demitasse coffee. Fill rest of the way with brandy. The brandy will rise to the top, at which time it should be ignited with a match, burned for several seconds, and stirred well before serving. (Serves 1.)

DANDELION COFFEE

Actually a coffee substitute which can be bought in a health food store. To prepare your own, take dandelion roots, wash them, trim leaves and then roast on a tray in the oven until brown, dry and very dark. Grind as ordinary coffee. Make like regular coffee, but use one teaspoon of grind to a pint of water.

ICED COFFEE

Iced coffee must be double the strength of regular hot coffee, as the water from the ice cubes will weaken the brew.

VIENNESE FROST

3 cups very strong
   coffee
2 crushed cinnamon
   sticks
4 whole cloves
4 allspice berries
ice
simple syrup (liquid
   sugar)
whipped cream

Pour coffee over cinnamon, cloves and allspice. Let sit for one hour. Strain and pour into tall glasses filled with ice. Sweeten with syrup and top with whipped cream.
(Serves 2.)

HAWAII FROST

1 cup strong cold
   coffee
½ cup chilled pine-
   apple juice
½ pint soft ice cream
   (select to taste)

Place all ingredients in blender and mix at low speed until smooth and foamy. Pour into tall glasses. (Serves 2.)

COFFEE NECTAR

1 cup strong cold coffee ½ pint coffee ice cream 1½ teaspoons angostura bitters	Blend all ingredients at low speed until smooth and creamy. Serve in tall glasses. (Serves 2.)

ICED COFFEE TROPICAL

finely chopped ice ¾ measuring cup very strong cold coffee 1 rounded tablespoon fine granulated sugar	Fill blender half full of ice, add other ingredients and mix at low speed until thick and creamy. (Serves 2.)

HONEY ICED COFFEE

ice 2 cups very strong cold coffee honey whipped cream cinnamon nutmeg	Fill two tall glasses with ice. Pour coffee over ice. Serve with honey and top with whipped cream. Sprinkle cinnamon and nutmeg on top. (Serves 2.)

TROPICANA CAFÉ

2 cups strong cold
  coffee
½ teaspoon rum
  flavoring
¼ cup light cream
sparkling water
simple syrup

Combine coffee, rum
flavoring and cream.
Chill well and pour into
three tall glasses. Fill
glasses with ice-cold
sparkling water. Stir
and sweeten with simple
syrup. (Serves 3.)

COFFEE EGGNOG

¾ cup sugar
1½ cups boiling water
1 cup ground coffee
5 egg yolks

1¼ quarts milk
5 egg whites
nutmeg

Add sugar to boiling water and stir until dissolved. Let
come to a boil. Remove from heat, add coffee, stir well,
cover, and let stand for 15 minutes. Let drip through two
thicknesses of wet cheesecloth placed in a strainer, and
then cool. Beat egg yolks and slowly stir in coffee syrup.
Add milk and blend well. Beat egg whites well and fold
in. Pour into a punch bowl. Serve in punch cups and
sprinkle with nutmeg. (Serves about 20.)

MOCHA FROSTED

1¼ cups strong cold
  coffee
2½ tablespoons
  chocolate syrup
½ pint coffee ice
  cream

Place all ingredients in
blender and mix at low
speed until smooth.
(Serves 2.)

BANANA COFFEE

1 ripe banana, sliced
¼ pint coffee ice cream
¼ cup light cream
⅛ teaspoon almond
  extract

1½ teaspoons instant
  coffee
¼ teaspoon lemon
  juice
1½ teaspoons sugar

Combine all ingredients in blender and whip until thick
and foamy. Pour into glasses or mugs. (Serves 2.)

PEANUT-BUTTER CAFÉ

½ cup extra-strong cold
  coffee
1 tablespoon powdered
  milk
½ heaping tablespoon
  peanut butter

1½ tablespoons sugar
½ cup crushed ice

Blend at high speed until all ingredients are mixed well
and the drink becomes foamy. Serve in a tall glass.
(Serves 1.)

COFFEE-ICE-CREAM SODA

1½ cups strong
  cold coffee
½ cup light cream
½ cup sugar syrup
  or light corn syrup
1 pint coffee ice cream
sparkling water

Mix the coffee, cream and
syrup well. Pour into tall
glasses. Add a scoop of
ice cream to each glass
and fill with ice-cold
sparkling water. (Serves
4.)

COFFEE COINTREAU

1 teaspoon grated
  lemon peel
1 jigger Cointreau
1 cup very hot coffee

Combine all ingredients.
(Serves 1.)

COFFEE GROG

peel of ½ orange, cut
  into strips
peel of ½ lemon, cut into
  strips
2 cinnamon sticks
1 teaspoon whole cloves
¼ cup sugar

2 ounces chocolate
  syrup
1 quart strong coffee
¼ teaspoon anise
  flavoring
vanilla ice cream or
  whipped cream

Combine all ingredients except ice cream in a saucepan.
Simmer for 15 minutes. Fill small cups or mugs two-thirds
full. Float vanilla ice cream or whipped cream on top.
(Serves 6.)

CAFÉ DE BELGIQUE

¼ teaspoon vanilla
½ cup heavy cream
1 egg white, beaten
  stiff
4 cups hot coffee

Combine vanilla and
cream. Whip. Blend with
egg white. Fill 4 cups one-
third full with cream mixture. Add hot coffee.
(Serves 4.)

PINEAPPLE COFFEE

½ cup extra-strong
  cold coffee
½ cup cracked ice
1 tablespoon sugar
¼ cup pineapple
  juice

In a blender whip ingredients at high speed until foamy. Serve in tall glasses. Garnish with pineapple cubes on toothpicks. (Serves 2.)

SPICY COFFEE

½ cup extra-strong
  cold coffee
½ cup cracked ice
1 tablespoon sugar
½ tablespoon lemon
  juice
dash ground cinnamon

Place all ingredients in blender and whip at high speed until foamy. Serve in tall glasses with a slice of lemon on the edge of glass. (Serves 2.)

VIENNESE SPICED COFFEE

1½ cups extra-strong
  coffee, very hot
2 whole cloves
2 allspice berries
1 cinnamon stick,
  chopped
whipped cream
nutmeg

Pour hot coffee over cloves, allspice and pieces of cinnamon. Simmer for 15 minutes. Strain. Pour into tall glasses or mugs. Top with whipped cream and nutmeg. Serve with sugar and sticks of cinnamon. (Serves 3.)

POSTUM

A coffee surrogate made of wheat grain, molasses and bran. These ingredients are roasted and extracted to make a beverage with a caramel flavor.

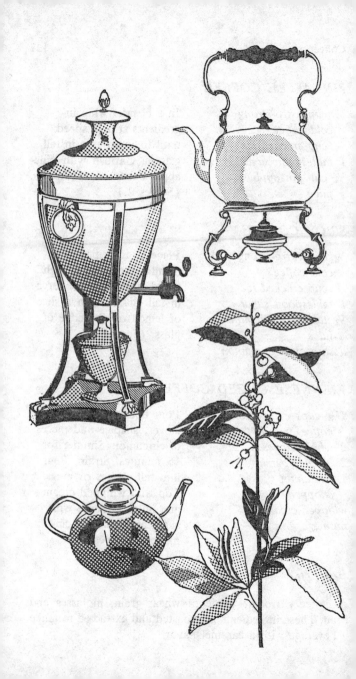

TEA

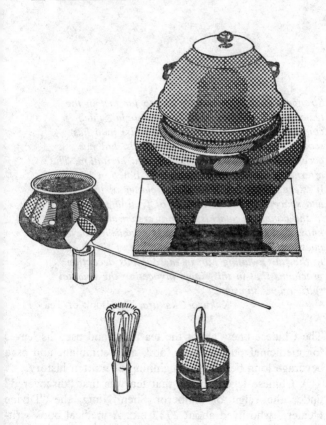

The Chinese have ... the ... and the ...
the original ... and ... culture, and each
village in ... has its own ... history.
A small ... of ... tea ... that changes ...
little one ... is or ... everyday, the Chinese
... who ... share ... are ... of some ...
... would ... prepare ... to ... could the day ...
... To ... across the Chinese ceremonies. Even
... will ... be ... by ... preventing of ...

ORIGINS

*Strangely enough, humanity has so far met in the
tea-cup. It is the only Asiatic ceremonial which
commands universal esteem. The white man has
scoffed at our religion and our morals, but has
accepted the brown beverage without hesitation. The
afternoon tea is now an important function in
Western society. In the delicate clatter of trays
and saucers, in the soft rustle of feminine hospitality,
in the common catechism about cream and sugar, we
know that the Worship of Tea is established beyond
question. The philosophic resignation of the guest
to the fate awaiting him in the dubious decoction
proclaims that in this single invocation the oriental
spirit reigns supreme.*

—*Kakuzo Okakura*, The Book of Tea

The Chinese knew about the tea plant and used its leaves
for medicinal purposes, as food, as a stimulant and as a
beverage long before the beginning of written history.

A Chinese legend holds that tea was first "discovered"
under the reign of Emperor Shen Nung, the "Divine
Healer," who lived about 2737 B.C. A medical book written under the emperor's name some two thousand years
after he lived records the following comments: "Bitter
t'u is called *ch'a, hsuan,* and *yu*. It grows in the valleys,

by the streams, and on the hills of Ichow, and does not perish in severe winter. It is gathered on the third day of the third month and then dried." The book goes on to mention that the tea leaf is "good for tumors or abscesses that come about the head, or for ailments of the bladder. It dissipates heat caused by phlegms, or inflammation of the chest. It quenches thirst. It lessens desire for sleep. It gladdens and cheers the heart."

The first use of the tea plant as a beverage was noted during the fourth century A.D. in a Chinese dictionary, which stated that the leaves were picked and made into cakes. The cakes were then roasted until reddish in color, pounded into tiny pieces and placed in a pot. Boiling water was poured over them and onion, ginger and orange were added.

At this time tea was still considered a medicine. It was not consumed for pleasure until 600 A.D., when the poet Chuang Meng-Yen wrote: "Fragrant t'u superimposes the six passions (content and anger, sorrow and joy, like and dislike); the taste for it spreads over the nine districts [the entire kingdom]." This taste for tea created great commercial activity and resulted in the commissioning of an encyclopedia of tea, the *Ch'a Ching* (Tea Classic) in 780 A.D. by the poet Lu Yu. This work covered all aspects of tea cultivation and preparation and is still consulted to-day for information regarding the ancient practices.

Tea made its entrance into Japan about 593 A.D. during the reign of Prince Shotoku. It was imported along with Chinese civilization, art and religion (Buddhism).

Japanese mythology credits the origin of tea in China to Bodhidharma. It is related that this Buddhist saint, when overcome with sleep during his meditations, cut off his eyelids and threw them on the ground, where they took root and grew as tea plants.

From the time it was introduced until the thirteenth century, tea was restricted to priests and members of the nobility. This changed around the year 1191 with the publication of the first popular Japanese work on tea by the Buddhist abbot Yeigai, who proclaimed tea "a divine remedy and a supreme gift of heaven for preserving human life."

🌸 INTRODUCTION TO THE WEST

The first reports of tea reached Europe in 1560 from a Portuguese missionary priest who wrote: "Whatsoever person or persons come to anyman's house of quality, he hath a custome to offer him . . . a kind of drinke called ch'a, which is somewhat bitter, red, and medicinall, which they are want to make with a certayne concoction of herbs."

Ships of the Dutch East India Company reached the islands off the coast of Japan in 1609, whence they returned with the first teas for Europe. In 1618, the Russian court in Moscow received a gift of several chests which had been brought overland by the Chinese ambassador. Eighteen months were required for the journey, which was made in the hopes of creating a demand for the product in Russia.

Around 1650, tea was first imported commercially to England. Prior to that time, according to the famous 1660 broadside advertisement of coffee-house owner Thomas Garway, the leaf and drink had been used only "as a regalia in high treatments and entertainments, and presents made thereof to princes and grandees."

Garway's copy states that "the leaf is of such known vertues, that those very Nations famous for Antiquitym

Knowledge, and Wisdom, do frequently sell it among
themselves for twice its weight in silver, and the high
estimation of the Drink made therewith both occasioned
an inquiry into the nature thereof amongst the most intelligent persons of all Nations that have travelled in those
parts, who after exact Tryal and Experience by all ways
imaginable, have commended it to the use of their several
Countries for its Vertues and Operations."

Garway proceeds to list dozens of "particular Vertues,"
some of which follow:

It maketh the body active and lusty.
It helpeth the Headache, giddiness, and heaviness thereof.
It removeth obstructions of the Spleen.
It (being prepared with milk and water) strengtheneth the
  inward parts, and prevents Consumptions, and power-
  fully assuageth the pain of the bowels.
It is good for Colds, Dropsies and Scurveys, if properly
  infused, purging the Blood by sweat and urine, and ex-
  pelleth infection.

By the eighteenth century, tea was firmly ensconced as
the English national beverage.

The United States first imported tea around 1650,
when the more elegant settlers of New Amsterdam paid
$30 to $50 per pound for it. The proper hostess would
brew several different kinds of tea in different pots for
her guests. Saffron or peach leaves were used as flavorings.

The beverage made its way through the colonies with
varying degrees of success. The problem was that it is
not obvious how to make tea. All methods are inventions.
In Salem, Massachusetts, the early settlers had little idea
of what to do with tea leaves. They boiled them for a
long time, which produced a bitter brew, then salted them
and ate them with butter.

By 1674 New Amsterdam had been renamed New
York. The change brought with it English culture, refine-

ment and customs. Within a few years, ladies would go to parties carrying their own teacups, saucers and spoons. Special "tea water" pumps were erected by the Corporation of New York, which ensured that the purest water possible could be obtained. This water was then carted through the streets of New York by "tea water" peddlers.

One hundred years later, in 1767, the British government put a tax on the tea used by American colonists. The colonists first boycotted tea and then brought the situation to a head in December, 1773, when a group of Bostonians, dressed as Indians, boarded an English vessel and dumped three hundred chests of tea overboard. This act, which eventually led to war, made America a non-tea-drinking nation for many years.

THE TEA PLANT

Tea is the dried leaf of an evergreen plant, a member of the camellia family. The seeds are obtained by allowing certain tea trees to grow until they reach a height of about twenty feet. During the blooming season, the tree is covered by small white sweet-smelling flowers from which hazelnutlike seeds develop.

These seeds are laid out six inches apart and grown to cutting size. After about a year they are removed to tea "gardens" or "estates." The young plants are not allowed to grow over five feet; they resemble bushes rather than the trees from which their seeds are gathered. The aim is to create a thicker plant and enable pickers to work easily by hand.

In three to five years, the plant produces new leaves which are known as the "flush." This consists of two new leaves and a bud. The bud is picked by hand, and the older leaves on the bottom are not taken.

VARIETIES

Teas are grown in Ceylon, China, India, Japan, Java, Sumatra and Taiwan. There are over three thousand varieties of the tea plant, and, like wines, they take their names from the districts in which they are grown.

The varieties, all of which come from the same bush, can be classified in three ways:

BLACK TEA   The leaves undergo a special process of oxidation (fermentation) that turns them black and produces a strong brew. Black teas are predominantly used today in the United States and other Western countries.

OOLONG TEA   The leaves are semi-oxidized, resulting in a half-brown, half-green color. The brew is light.

GREEN TEA   The leaves do not undergo the oxidation process and stay green.

For centuries, only green tea was known and used as a beverage. When the Western nations began to import teas from the Orient, they made long sea voyages, during which the tea leaves were subject to the elements. This led accidentally to the process of oxidation. Rather than lose their investment on an entire cargo of now "rotten" tea, the shippers went ahead and sold the "black" teas to Europeans who did not know any better. To this day, tea drinkers in the Orient cannot understand how people of Western nations can drink "rotted" teas. Black teas are not favored in the Orient, where green teas are the standard.

The better-known varieties within these three main classifications are:

BLACK TEAS

Assam (India): A high-grade India tea, grown in Assam province in Northeast India.

Darjeeling (India): The finest and most delicately flavored of the India teas. Grown in the Himalayas at the foot of Mount Everest.

Ceylon: The best-quality Ceylon teas are called "High Grown," which indicates growth at heights exceeding four thousand feet. The subtle teas from the district of Uva are considered best.

Keemun (China): A fine-grade tea of China congou type from Taiwan.

Lapsong Souchong (China): From the Lapsong district.

Earl Grey (Blend): A custom blend which has kept the name of the customer for whom it was originally intended.

English Breakfast (Blend): Originally the name applied to China congou teas. Now it is used for blends of black teas in which the China character dominates.

OOLONG TEAS

Taiwan oolong: A large-leaf semi-oxidized tea from Taiwan.

Jasmine: A delicately flavored tea, scented with white jasmine blossoms.

GREEN TEAS

Basket Fired (Japan): A light and gentle Japanese brew.

Gunpowder (Ceylon): A type of Ceylonese green tea in which each leaf is rolled into a small pellet.

PROCESSING

It takes long, patient processing to develop the color, fragrance and flavor of tea from the green leaf after it has been hand-picked. From that point, the leaves go through five stages of processing: withering, rolling, roll-breaking, fermenting and drying.

1. *withering:* The fresh green leaves are spread on racks and subjected to heated air to evaporate the moisture so the leaf will become soft and pliable. This process lasts up to a full day.
2. *rolling:* The pliable leaves are rolled on special machines to break up their cells and free the juices, which give tea its special flavor and aroma. This process helps to develop the essential oil of tea; a chemical change occurs when the juices that remain on the leaves are exposed to air.
3. *roll-breaking:* This is a sieve process in which the lumps from rolling are broken up through a coarse mesh. The tea leaves that fall through are then ready for the next step.
4. *fermenting (oxidation):* In cool, humid rooms, the leaves undergo further chemical change through absorption of oxygen. During this fermenting process, the leaves turn from green to a bright copper. In making green teas, this process is omitted. For oolong tea, the

leaves are partially fermented. Fermentation is the only
difference between black, oolong and green teas.

5. *drying* (*firing*): The leaves are placed on moving trays
which pass through blasts of hot air that dry them without scorching. This process is necessary to end the
fermentation and dry the leaves evenly.

GRADES

After the plain tea leaves are processed into black, oolong
or green tea, they are graded and sorted for commercial
distribution. The processed leaves are mixed together and
go through sieves with graduated meshes which divide
them into leaf grades and broken grades. These grades
relate *only* to size. A term such as "orange pekoe" does
not refer to a variety of tea, or to its color, but merely
to the size of the tea leaves.

LEAF GRADES   These are made of the larger leaves
left after the broken grades have been sifted out. In brewing, the flavor, aroma and color come out of leaf grades
more slowly than out of broken grades. For black tea,
the leaf grades, from largest to smallest, are

Orange Pekoe: Long, thin, wiry leaves, sometimes including yellow tips or bud leaves.
Pekoe: The leaves of this grade are shorter and not so wiry
as orange pekoe. Makes a darker tea.
Souchong: A round leaf which makes a pale tea.

BROKEN GRADES   These represent about 80 percent
of the total crop. They make a dark, strong tea and are
the choice of most countries outside Continental Europe
and South America. This is the "tea bag" grade, which
is by far the most popular in the United States.

Broken Orange Pekoe: Much smaller than any of the leaf
grades and usually containing yellow tips. The liquors

have a good color and strength in the cup and are the mainstay of a blend.

Broken Pekoe: Slightly larger than broken orange pekoe with less color in the cup. Useful as a filler in the blend.

Broken Pekoe Souchong: A little larger than broken pekoe and therefore lighter in the cup. Also used as a filler.

Fannings: Much smaller than broken orange pekoe. Its main virtues are quick brewing and strong color in the cup.

Dust: The smallest grade produced. Very useful for quick brewing of a strong cup of tea. Used only in blends of similar-sized leaves.

There are similar gradings for green teas. From largest to smallest, they are gunpowder, pea leaf, imperial, young hyson and hyson.

UNITED STATES IMPORTS

Processed and graded teas are sold at auctions in London, Amsterdam, Calcutta and Colombo (Ceylon). The teas purchased by agents of United States companies arrive in aluminum-foil-lined tea chests and are placed in bonded warehouses where they await approval by the U.S. Board of Tea Experts, a six-member body nominated by both government and industry. Once approved, the teas are removed to packagers. In commercial tea-bag blends, some companies use up to twenty or more varieties in an attempt to maintain a constant quality. These blends are created and maintained by the fabled "tea-tasters," who are able to identify up to 1,500 different teas.

As with coffees, it makes good sense to shop for specific varieties and sample them all to develop your own personal taste. Most of the varieties previously mentioned are available in the more sophisticated food stores.

The tea bag, a rather recent innovation, does nothing except to simplify tea-making, yet it does seem to detract from the ritualistic preparation of a brew whose history is so related to such customs. In this country, tea is available either loose, in tea bags or as powder. Instant teas are also available as a concentrated form of brewed tea from which the water has been removed through a drying process.

🌺 MAKING TEA

The art of making tea has changed little since 780 A.D., when the *Ch'a Ching* prescribed the proper utensils, preparation and serving of tea.

Follow these simple instructions:

(1) Use tea leaves in loose form, as the paper in tea bags can subtly alter the delicate flavor.

(2) Use a teapot of china or earthenware. Preheat it by rinsing it out with scalding-hot water. This helps to keep the teapot hot during brewing.

(3) Place one teaspoon of leaves in the teapot for every cup of water. To avoid the eventual bother of using a strainer, the leaves may first be put in a small metal tea ball which is placed in the teapot and later removed.

(4) Always use fresh cold water for boiling.

(5) Add water that has *only just been brought to a full boil*. Cover and steep no less than four minutes (longer for a stronger brew). For a weaker tea, add hot water to the full-strength brew *after* the full brewing period.

(6) Don't judge the strength of the tea by its ⌐ teas brew light, some dark. Brew by *'*

(7) Stir the tea before pouring to ⌐ strong. Circulating the brew

add to the flavor of the tea. If the tea has to stand for any length of time, strain the liquid from the leaves (or remove tea ball).

(8) Do not reheat tea after it has brewed. Serve immediately.

(9) As an additive always use milk instead of cream in order to let the true flavor come out. Make sure the milk is kept at room temperature for serving.

(10) The making of tea is an ancient ritual. Good tea is a social rite and should always be prepared in the presence of guests.

CAFFEINE AND TANNIN IN TEA Properly made tea helps to create a relaxed, refreshed feeling. This is due to the caffeine and tannin. Unlike that in coffee, however, the caffeine in tea does not cause negative side effects like overnervousness and insomnia.

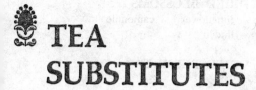

TEA SUBSTITUTES

There are numerous surrogates for the tea leaf, among them countless different kinds of flowers and herbs. For instance, besides the leaves of the tea shrub, the flowers are sometimes dried and a beverage made from them in the same way in which the leaves are brewed.

Brazilian or Paraguayan tea, called maté, is actually not tea at all but is made from the dried leaves of the *Ilex paraguariensis* shrub.

Herb "teas" have always been popular remedies, and in Europe they are still prescribed by doctors. Herb teas are generally brewed the same way as tea leaves. Use two teaspoons per cup of boiling water. If fresh herbs are used, double the quantity. Mineral-rich herb teas may be made with any of the following ingredients, alone or in any desired combination:

FRESH OR DRIED LEAVES

alfalfa	blackberry	sage
oat straw	parsley	costmary
shavegrass	hyssop	balm
rue	celery	comfrey
blueberry	mint	

FRESH OR DRIED BLOSSOMS

clover   limeflower   camomile
elderberry   linden

FRESH OR DRIED BERRIES

rose hips

SEEDS

fenugreek   celery   caraway
alfalfa   fennel   coriander
anise   dill

ROOT

licorice

Herb teas may also be combined with fresh fruit juices.
They can be served plain or flavored with powdered fruit
rind, honey or lemon juice.

TEAS & TEA BEVERAGES

ASSAM TEAS

Black India tea. Golden-tipped tea has a strong, full-bodied, rich flavor. Brew six minutes.

CEYLON ORANGE PEKOE TEA

Appealing flavor, aroma and strength in this black tea. Ceylon teas brew faster than varieties grown farther away from the equator. Perfect with milk or a slice of lemon.

DARJEELING TEA

Highly prized by tea connoisseurs. The golden liquor of Darjeeling should be sipped and treated as a wine.
  Darjeeling should be brewed about seven minutes.

EARL GREY BLEND

A black-tea blend of Darjeeling and Keemun, China. Well-scented with orange. Fragrant, with a delicate flavor.

ENGLISH AFTERNOON TEA

A black-tea blend of quality Ceylon teas.

ENGLISH BREAKFAST

A rich, hearty, full-bodied black-tea blend. Combines the strength and color of India tea with flavor of Ceylon tea

GEORGIA BLEND

Lemon-scented black tea that is good either iced or hot

IRISH BREAKFAST

A medium-strong blend of Ceylon and India black teas. Ideal for drinkers who like a pungent brew.

KEEMUN TEA

Black Chinese tea, fine and smooth. Most celebrated of the China teas. Known for its fragrance and exceptionally delicate flavor.

LAPSONG SOUCHONG

Smoky flavor and aroma with extremely strong taste. Often mixed with Assam and Ceylon teas. Appreciated by connoisseurs dating back to the great mandarins of ancient China.

TAIWAN OOLONG

Natural fruity flavor with the aroma of ripe peaches. Light in color.

JASMINE BLEND

Combination of fine Ceylon orange pekoes and jasmine teas. Delicious flavor of the jasmine-scented blossoms. An unusual China tea.

GREEN GUNPOWDER

Has appearance of old Chinese gunpowder. Use this tea as a flavoring with a black tea. Brews as a clear, fragrant liquor.

JAPANESE UNCOLORED GREEN TEA

Known as the white wine of teas.

SPIDER LEG TEA

A Japanese green tea so named because of the long thin leaves. Once very popular, not used widely now.

YOUNG HYSON

A rare high-quality Chinese green tea.

MINT TEA

Choice Ceylons blended with rubbed mint.

ORANGE SPICE TEA

Orange peel and dashes of spices blended with high-grade Ceylons.

PALM SPRINGS BLEND

A fine blend of green and semi-green teas much the same
as the Queen Victoria Blend, minus the smoky flavor.

QUEEN VICTORIA BLEND

Considered one of the world's finest teas. A smoky flavor.

RUSSIAN CARAVAN BLEND

A blend of the best China teas. It gets its name from the
days when camel caravans brought tea from China to
Europe in overland journeys, starting during the reign of
Empress Elizabeth in 1753.

CAMOMILE TEA

Dried camomile blossoms are used. Use two teaspoons
per cup of boiling water.

MATÉ

Paraguayan or Brazilian "tea," made from the dried leaves
of *Ilex paraguariensis* (shrub). Prepared in a small silver-
mounted calabash about the size of a large orange, with
the top open. Sugar and a little water are placed in the
container, the maté is added, and finally the vessel is filled
to the brim with boiling water and heated milk. The beverage is then consumed in a ritual which involves the use
of a small tube, six to seven inches long, formed of either
metal or reed. The maté is sucked up through this tube
called a *bombilla,* which is passed from hand to hand.

APPLE TEA

Dry ripe-apple parings either in the sun or a warm (not hot) oven. Use half a handful of dried parings per cup of boiling water. Serve with a slice of lemon.

BALM TEA

12 sprigs lemon balm	6 cloves
2 teaspoons sugar	juice of ½ lemon

Place lemon balm, sugar, cloves and lemon juice in a jar. Pour one pint of boiling water over ingredients. Cover and let brew for a minimum of 5 minutes. Strain and serve. (Serves 2.)

CARROT AND CELERY TEA

1 tablespoon grated carrot	Prepare as tea, using one cup of boiling water.
1 tablespoon grated celery	(Serves 1.)
2 teaspoons oatmeal	

BEET AND CUCUMBER TEA

1 tablespoon shredded beets	Prepare as tea, using one cup of boiling water.
1 tablespoon shredded cucumbers	(Serves 1.)

DANDELION-FLOWER TEA

1 cup dandelion petals
juice of ½ lemon
1 tablespoon honey
¾ pint boiling water

Combine petals, lemon
and honey. Pour boiling
water over these in-
gredients. Cover and brew
until cool. Serve cold.
(Serves 2.)

FRESH MINT TEA

Using chopped fresh mint, make as tea, using 2 teaspoons
per cup of boiling water. Serve with honey and lemon
slices. Good for digestion and nervous headaches.

HOT SPICED TEA

1 quart water
2 tablespoons loose tea
¼ stick cinnamon
¼ teaspoon whole cloves

¼ cup sugar
3 tablespoons lemon
    juice
¼ cup orange juice

Boil water and pour over tea, cinnamon and cloves. Cover
and let brew for five minutes. Stir and strain. Add sugar
and stir until dissolved. Add lemon and orange juice. To
reheat, place over low heat and do not boil. Garnish with
lemon slices. (Serves 5.)

PEPPERMINT TEA

Place ½ teaspoon of fresh peppermint in teapot. Add
two cups boiling water and brew for ten minutes.

RAISIN-BRAN TEA

15 chopped raisins
3 tablespoons bran
1 pint boiling water

Soak raisins and bran for 8 hours in one pint of boiling water. Strain and drink hot or cold. Very high in iron. (Serves 2.)

ROSE-HIP TEA

½ cup rose hips
1 quart water

Boil together for an hour. Strain and serve hot or cold. Very high in vitamin C. (Serves 3.)

ROSE-PETAL TEA

2 teaspoons red rose petals
2 teaspoons lavender flowers
2 teaspoons rosemary needles

Brew in 3 cups boiling water for no less than 5 minutes. (Serves 3–4.)

INSTANT TEA

The powder is prepared by using a highly concentrated brew of tea from which the water is removed by a drying process. The powder dissolves instantly in water, hot or cold.

HOT INSTANT One level teaspoon to a cup. Two level tablespoons for each quart.

ICED INSTANT One rounded teaspoon for each six-ounce glass of cold water. Two rounded tablespoons for each quart of cold water.

ICED TEA

Make twice as strong as hot tea. When refrigerated, iced tea may cloud. It is best kept out of the refrigerator. To restore the color after clouding, add a little boiling water.

Lemon or orange slices can be frozen to use instead of ice cubes. Tiny pieces of mint frozen in ice cubes make an attractive addition to lemon iced tea.